TONY ELLIOTT

A MODERN APPROACH TO GOALKEEPING

Best Wishes

Written by: Adam Woodage
Designed by: Adam Woodage
Covers by: Miklos Zsengeller
Printed and bound by: GOMER Printing
ISBN: 978-0-9935165-9-7

A catalogue record for this book is available from the British Library.

Photo Coverage

To the best of our knowledge, all photos contained within this book are either of the property of Tony Elliott or with their permission and right to be reproduced within this publication.

Every effort has been made to trace and contact copyright holders where applicable. If there are any inadvertent omissions we apologise to those concerned, and ask that you contact us so that we can correct any oversight as soon as possible. The contact details are given below:

AW Publications
6 Chaffinch
Watermead
Aylesbury
Bucks HP19 0GQ

We thank you for your cooperation and understanding within this matter.

A LIFETIME IN THE GAME

Head of International Youth Goalkeeping
England women's football (WU15-WU20)

Head of Goalkeeping
England men's senior futsal squad

Joint Head Coach
England women's deaf futsal squad

Head of Goalkeeping
England men's senior B1 blind football squad

Head of Goalkeeping
England men's senior CP seven-a-side football squad

Head of Goalkeeping
GB men's senior CP seven-a side football squad

CONTINUED

FA Goalkeeping Level 1 & 2
Course tutor/assessor

FA Futsal Level 1
Course Tutor

FA Goalkeeping for Futsal
Workshop creator/tutor

FA Goalkeeping Conference (2013-2016)
Futsal & disability football goalkeeping workshops

Ex-Professional Goalkeeper (1987-2000)
6 clubs and approx. 250 league & cup appearances

CONTENTS

SESSION DELIVERY   175

CASE STUDIES   217

STILL HUNGRY FOR MORE?   256

DEDICATIONS

To my soul mate and long suffering wife, Tracy: without you, none of this would have meaning as you are my purpose and my drive in life. Thank you for your belief in me and for your willingness to sacrifice so much time together in allowing me to pursue my dreams. It is you that keeps the family unit together when we are apart so often and for that I am eternally grateful. To you and our children I dedicate my first publication as you deserve the most credit for always pushing me and giving me the inspiration to be the best I can be every day. I love you. X

To our four amazing children, Joshua, Robbie, Bruckman and Dharma. You are the lights of my life and you have all become such wonderful young people. I do what I do for you and I hope that you are as proud of me as I am of you. You bring so much joy into our lives and I cherish the moment that you were all brought into this world. Love Dad. X

THANK YOUS

To my parents, Bob and Jean, thank you for bringing me into this world. You have always been there for me and offered me the best advice. You gave me the most fantastic upbringing that has given me the platform to be the man, husband and father that I am today.

You stood by me through the tough times during my career and I know that the good times I have experienced as a player and now a coach, have given you so much pleasure and that is your reward for the dedication to my career that you have always shown. I love you both very much and thank you.

To the rest of my family and closest friends, thanks for being there and being part of my journey. I'm indebted to your support and I hope you enjoy the read!

For my final thank you, I will mention a dear friend who shall be known to those close to me as Nanny. Over the past 20 years, Nanny was a part of my family's life and, like me, she was an avid reader and she and I spent many an afternoon discussing my latest purchase (much to the joy of my wife Tracy and our friend Joni!). Nanny was so proud of me for being the caring man that I am and she made it clear to the two ladies that I was very much her blue-eyed boy!

Sadly, Nanny passed away recently and left a big gap in our lives, she was aware that I was in the process of putting together this book and this made her very proud. I'd like to think that she is smiling now, wherever she is, in the knowledge that her 'blue-eyed boy' had stuck to task and seen the job through.

Nanny, I miss our chats and I know you will be smiling over me now in whatever part of the universe you are currently blessing. Love Tone.

There are so many individuals that have played a part in my life and evolution as a person, player and coach. I hope that if I miss out anyone by name then please don't take it personally but I only have limited space. I could fill a book with you all!

ACKNOWLEDGEMENTS

Some will never know how much of a contribution they have made along my life path and how much they have helped to mould and shape me by me merely having contact with them. I have been truly blessed to spend precious moments with so many that have given me so much learning and knowledge, combined with life skills, that have helped propel me forward on my journey.

Special mentions go out to my futsal family brothers: Pete Sturgess, Graeme Dell and Mike Skubala. You're depth of knowledge of the game has not only inspired me, but a nation of new futsal enthusiasts who now recognise what a fantastic sport futsal truly is and are well and truly 'on the bus'. They are helping give the sport the standing it deserves in this country. I thank you for your support and for giving me the opportunity to be part of its growth in the UK.

Others who have come into my life and left an indelible impression on me in their own unique way to name but a few are my dear friends Keith Mayer, you are my brother from another mother and I cherish our friendship. Thank you for your guidance, advice and our lengthy chats.

Keith Webb: our journey to Rio was at times challenging, filled with moments when we had to dig deep to find inspiration to drive the boys to be the best they could be to get them to the holy grail. Most of all, my friend, it was a monumental achievement to get as close as we did, always against the odds but graced with a laugh and a smile as we enjoyed each other's company so much. Forever honoured to have been your wingman and would do it all again if ever you asked me to!

Jeff Davis and James Watkins: you gave me the opportunity to work in the formats of the game that have become so dear to me and for that I will be forever grateful. You are gentlemen.

Mark Leather: my buddy from the get go. Many a laugh was had in those early futsal days and to this day we always remember the fun we had on the road around Europe and on home soil. Forever yours, Sarge!

Adam: you are a true inspiration to all young people of this world, showing that if you really want to achieve something and believe in it, anything is possible. I thank you from the heart for your dedication to this book and the way in which you have conducted yourself throughout the process; you are a man way ahead of your years. Thank you, dear friend, you are a special young man.

Derek Birrell: you'll probably tell me off for doing this, but on behalf of Adam and myself, our deepest gratitude to you for your wonderful gesture. The free session for you and the band is yours whenever you fancy a kick about!!

Finally, to those close to me who I may have missed, you are all special in your own way and I am grateful for you being in my life and I know you have all played a part in some way on my journey. You know who you are!!

Enjoy,
Tony

FOREWORD
PETER STURGESS

It has been my pleasure to work with Tony for almost eight years with the England senior men's futsal squad. During that time, he researched, studied and experimented with his own unique interpretation of the role of the futsal goalkeeper. In a short period of time he elevated our goalkeepers to another level of performance and understanding. This is Tony: diligent, hard working, and yet incredibly creative in his thoughts and ideas. He was a massive part of the success of the team and because he applies this to everything he does I know he will continue to develop and influence coaches in a very positive way. There are some people who come into your life and leave a permanent mark on you. Tony was, and is, one of those people. His passion for helping and developing both people and players shines through in the way that he approaches his work as a coach and coach educator. I know the same kind of commitment, passion and attention to detail will shine through in the pages that follow allowing Tony to leave an indelible mark upon your development as a coach.

Enjoy the read,

Pete.

INTRODUCTION
TONY ELLIOTT

I love the game of football; have done ever since I could walk. My dream as a child was to firstly be a professional footballer but then to be able to play for my beloved Birmingham City, both of which I achieved. My career as a professional player spanned nearly 14 years before I sustained the back injury that put an end to me being athletic enough to play at the very top level. As I couldn't play anymore, I knew that my only way of being involved in the sport that I loved was to turn my hand to coaching.

During my playing and coaching career to date, I have had the honour of representing my country at schoolboy and youth level, as well as having the opportunity to be coached by or work alongside some fantastic individuals from within the game such as Mike Kelly, Peter Shilton, Neville Southall,

Jim Barron, Alan Hodgkinson, Joe Corrigan, Mick Wadsworth, Simon Smith, Martin Thomas, Tony Coton, Graeme Dell and Pete Sturgess to name a very non-exhaustive list.

Over the years, I have been blessed with so many wonderful opportunities, working for two of the biggest football clubs in the world: Liverpool FC and Manchester City FC. I've coached as both goalkeeper and assistant coach at professional club-level, semi-professional-level, international-level and worked with and tutored hundreds if not thousands of coaches and players at grassroots-level.

I have loved every second of being in a position to work for The FA, representing my country around the world over the last 10 years and I'm truly humbled by the fact that I still today work across numerous squads simultaneously.

My biggest achievement is being one of only what may be described as a handful of people to have worked across five different formats of the game, namely: men's football, women's football, futsal, blind football and cerebral palsy football. Each in its own way unique, all are special to me and I'm blessed to have had the opportunity to develop myself through immersion in each format and attempting to us those learnings and findings to aid the development of players and coaches from all five formats!

Family Influences

I have my Father, Bob, and my mother, Jean, to thank for my introduction into the footballing world, when over a short period of time during my early years I was thrust into a world of amateur men's senior Sunday League team training sessions and also Junior School football competition in my home city of Birmingham. My talent was raw but I think those close to me always knew that I was only ever destined for a future in the game because of my passion and love for the sport (and that I wasn't particularly any good at anything else!!)

The sheer love, devotion and dedication to my wife Tracy and our four angels, Joshua, Robbie, Bruckman and Dharma are my life purpose and the reason why I have dedicated so much time away from them over the years in my pursuit of forging a career most importantly to care for them but also to do something that I just love doing and will do until I'm physically no longer capable – coach within the game in whatever format that may be!

Why The Book

So: why was I compelled to put this book together? Simple – It's all about caring and sharing!

I care deeply about the betterment and the development

of people and I truly believe that by sharing my story, the knowledge I have accrued over my years in sport and the wonderful life experiences that I have been so lucky to have then I truly know that the book will tick all of those boxes.

My wish is that others learn from some mistakes that I have made along the way but also to recognise that life often presents opportunities in front of you and it's the moments of decision that define us one way or another and that sometimes you just got to go with your heart and not your head: put faith and trust in yourself to get the job done and come out the other side smiling!

Modern Goalkeeping

The world of goalkeeping is constantly evolving. The back-pass rule was the catalyst for change within the game of football and the goalkeeper's role has been in constant flux ever since. The nature and speed of the game is rapidly changing, whilst tactical and strategical advances made within the coaching world are forever challenging the modern goalkeeper to become ever more involved in the game not just technically but in a completely holistic way.

The modern goalkeeper must now be fully equipped to not only be the guardian of the goal but also to be the overload or extra player when the team have possession of the ball and are looking to exploit defensive weakness in the opposition before them.

Therefore, the modern goalkeeper coach must also now equip themselves with the understanding and new knowledge of the role of the goalkeeper in order to develop each individual placed under their tutelage, to the expected levels of all round competency and consistent performance.

How to use this book

I truly believe that you, the reader of this book, will be in a better place as a coach and have a more open mind, not only in terms of the way you coach but also in the way in which you connect and care for each individual with whom you have contact with in your everyday lives as well as within your footballing circles.

Each aspect of the book will deliver a consistent message to you based on experiences from my personal and professional life both on and off the football field/futsal court and also from a journey filled with life's ups and downs and the challenges that we all face on a daily basis as we strive to make the world that we live in a much better place for us and the generations following in our footsteps.

Use its contents to guide, nurture, develop, drive, inspire and coach those that you feel can benefit in order for the message to be passed from generation to generation.

Enjoy the read and much love to you and those that you truly care for!

Section One

The journey into coaching

I

A BOYHOOD DREAM

Over the days, weeks and months that Tony and I have spent together, crafting the words that appear in front of you, Tony's love and desire for the game of football has bubbled to the forefront of nearly every conversation. Whether we be discussing the nuances of Cerebral Palsy goalkeeping, the evolution of the futsal block technique or building a syllabus for elite-level goalkeepers, I've consistently been struck by his passion for the game. This is a facet likely evolved from his early footballing days as a Birmingham City fan.

'Mainstream football was something exposed to me at quite a young age, if I think about it', says Tony. 'I started watching from the early 70s, as my dad and uncles were season ticket holders at Birmingham City FC. There were some incredible games in that period, with brilliant atmospheres and massive crowds: it was the era of Liverpool and Leeds: a wonderful time to experience the start of my footballing journey'.

Tony talks of how he would travel eagerly with family to catch a glimpse of the blues in action, with the atypical beauty of 20th century football underlining all of his early footballing memories. 'Without compromise, I'd be wearing my tracksuit as we made our way to the ground, and on our way we'd head to the local bakers, because I was a huge fan of the mince beef and onion pies that they sold. I was probably only six or seven at the time, but one of the most important parts of the experience, alongside the Bovril!, was the match-day programme. Everything was so open back in those days. Whilst I was sat, immersed in the opposition analysis, Dad and his friends would be having a drink at the bar, and others were smoking around them. They spoke so passionately about the team and club they loved. The canteen, the ground and the smells are still vivid in my mind so many years on.'

It wasn't necessarily just the teams during this period, though, that had Tony hooked on chasing a - more brown than white - ball around a sodden field for an hour and a half. 'Particularly, there, was a huge pot of goalkeeping talent during this period', he recalls, 'and I was lucky enough to hear about and really experience a great deal of it. Mike Kelly came up in conversation with my father as a youngster, and we used to chat about him a lot.' He would then transpire to be Tony's goalkeeper coach and mentor at Lilleshall, many years later.

When probed on whether Tony's exposure to such an array of goalkeeping talent was to contribute to his later career, he very firmly attested that he didn't believe in coincidences. 'If you think about my exposure to wonderful goalkeepers throughout the league over that initial period (the likes of Mike Kelly, Dave and Pete Latchford, Jim Montgomery, Jeff Wealands, Tony Coton and David Seaman), it was immense. Jimmy Rimmer was a great example of this. Obviously, he was in the European-cup-winning Villa side and I was a Birmingham fan, but I can't say that stopped me brining out a bag full of gloves to all of my games over a period of time.' It's clear that these goalkeeping idols had a tangible influence on the way Tony both played and perceived the game of football, even as a youngster making his first steps in the game.

Being his boyhood club, though, there was always going to be an affinity between Tony and Birmingham City, which he remembers with emotions of joy and nostalgia: 'My family, right up from my grandfather to my uncles and parents, were massive Birmingham fans and I'd always been fed the stories of great times at City, with some incredible goalkeepers. As a young boy, I was introduced to the team by going to games and watching them on a regular basis. The same as young child would be after immersion in an environment, I very quickly became a hugely passionate fan of Birmingham and a staunch blue nose!'

'That was me hooked and it was always my dream to play for them: I got the kits at Christmas and used to travel to as many away games as I could get to. By the age of 10 or 11, I was starting to imagine what it might be like to play for Birmingham City, and it was something that always sent shivers down my spine - what better could any youngster dream of?'

STEPPING STONES

However, Tony's first proper footballing experience would present itself well away from the realms of elite football, as he was invited to join the Catholic Community Centre Boy's football club, in his home city of Birmingham, through the school team. 'I think I was 8 years old playing for under 10s', remembers Tony. We used to get battered every week - absolutely ripped to shreds! - but I used to get Man of the Match awards left, right and centre because I just had so much to do. I remember the worst defeat we ever had was something like 14-0 and to me it didn't matter. I just loved playing, throwing myself around in the mud and being a goalkeeper. In some ways, it was great learning for me, even at that age.' He might not have noticed it for a good few years, but it could well be that these situations set Tony up to deal with later setbacks in his footballing career, as well as fostering an intrinsic love for the game.

'It taught me how to handle heavy defeats back-to-back, and to keep persisting without giving up. I spent a season with that team and we finished bottom of the league; I think we only won one game that year, but it was fantastic and I loved every minute of it.'

Following this season, Tony was approached by the manager from his own age group, two years younger: Brendan Flanagan. 'Brendan was a local coach involved in the club, running the under 9s team at the time that we crossed paths. He must have spoken to my uncle, Colin, who was also involved at that time with the older age groups. I started training with Brendan's team and straight away it was perfect: I loved the teammates, the activities we were doing and the general culture of the squad.'

After hearing how Brendan made Tony captain of the side, it is clear just quite how much of a footballing influence Brendan was on a young Tony and the impact he had on his future desire for the game. 'Brendan was instrumental, without a doubt. I hung on every word he said and had a lot of affinity for the man who kindled my burning desire for club football.'

'Sadly, he's not with us anymore and it was a big loss to his family and everybody involved in football at the Three Cs because there's a lot of history behind him and he was a very successful manager for the club. He was a major part in my development as a young goalkeeper and I think he was proud when I got selected from the recreational youth teams into the elite and academy setup (Tony was selected for the Castle Vale Boys Youth League representative squad as captain).

LATE DEVELOPER

Tony's forage into the academy setup, though, wouldn't follow for a few more years, even if the majority of his friends were attached to clubs by the age of 10 or 11. 'As I was a late developer, I wasn't picked up until the age of 13. I went through a period of playing really well, and was first spotted in a district game by an Aston Villa scout who wasn't even supposed to be watching me', he remarked. 'Unbeknownst to us, the opposition goalkeeper was already attached to Aston Villa, and the scout was watching to provide an update report to his coaches during the game. We won the match 3-0 and I'd had absolutely nothing to do all game until the last minute.'

'Stourbridge had an attack, with the ball falling to one of their players on the edge of the box. He volleyed it towards goal and hit it so sweetly, it was flying into the top corner. Somehow, though, I was equal to it, flinging myself towards the top of the goal and managing to get the faintest touch on the ball to tip it over the crossbar. I can remember vividly the gasps of amazements and surprise among the crowd watching, it was as if time had just stood still.' It transpired that this moment would prove to be the embryo of Tony's career as it's seen today, and certainly a pivotal turning point in his life journey.

When questioned on whether there was any involvement with 'luck' that afternoon, Tony had a firm response. 'It happened because it was meant to happen and was a crucial factor in the carving of my path for the future - I don't doubt that the same would've occurred in a parallel universe. Chance had little impact on it.' Whilst the save might have sent the rest of the fifty-strong contingency into an avid round of applause, Tony's father, Bob, was seemingly the only man in the crowd with two feet firmly planted on the floor: 'My dad, being my dad, walked with me after the match and said "Not a bad save, Son, I wasn't sure you were going to make that one", despite the fact it seemed to have the rest of the audience in captivation'.

It was during this walk, however, that Tony and his parents were approached by the mysterious, grey-haired scout, yielding the complementing trench jacket and notepad in hand. Inviting Tony to the Villa training complex, and unknowingly starting the plethora of explosions within his young career, the scout commended Tony on a save that he described as 'incomparable'. Even as an outsider looking into Tony's career, it can still be rather awe-inspiring to sit back and appreciate the pivotal importance that such fine moments can have on the career and journey of a professional within the game.

Maybe it's the random and varied nature of the system; maybe it's something more holistic than that. All that's clear is that the decisions that Tony would make (eventually signing as a schoolboy for his home-town club Birmingham City) were a distinct product of his early philosophies and views as a person. 'It's not fair to say that I regret not taking the opportunity to go and play for Manchester [United]', repels Tony, when asked whether interest from the worldwide super-club is something he wishes he'd pursued in more detail. 'It's always difficult when clubs are offering to relocate your family and take you on as a schoolboy apprentice, especially when they're a club as big as United are. One of the detractions for me, though, was the interference it would have had with the Lilleshall program, as well as the fact that I was a Birmingham fan and had always wanted to put on my home team's shirt on a match-day!'

Tony signed for Birmingham predominantly because he could play for them and partake in the Lilleshall programme in parallel, an opportunity he wasn't offered at too many other clubs.

However, his time as a Birmingham schoolboy wasn't the

most conventional. Not only was he developing in a time where specific goalkeeper coaching was absent from the academy design, but also because of his aforementioned commitments to the Lilleshall programme. 'The experience at Birmingham was a little bit strange, especially once I'd been training with them for so long before actually signing. It transpired that I didn't really spend too much time with the team, as it coincided with the Lilleshall schools' programme, which was a full-time, residential affair, so I only had the opportunity to be with the Birmingham squads during the holidays. Although I signed for Birmingham, I could be quite elusive at times!'

LILLESHALL

The decision to take up the offer of Lilleshall is one that Tony looks back on with great fondness: a major stepping stone, if you like, on the road to an FA-fuelled career that would span so many different national mechanisms. 'Lilleshall was an amazing experience', remembers Tony. 'There was a huge process to get there, with rigorous testing of thousands of players, over quite a large period of time. The trials started locally, before having two or three regional events, from which the best players would move forward to a set of national training sessions. There were three or four national trials, which were incredibly high quality, and the selectors were always whittling down the numbers from 60 to 40, then to 30, before finally they made the decision for the successful 25', remembers Tony, still with a glint of fear in his eye.

'It felt a little bit like some of the TV shows they have on nowadays, and I distinctly remember the agony and excitement involved in waiting for the letter to come through after each set of trials - it was a big part of The FA only to send letters. Luckily for me, every letter that I had was a positive one and I'll never forget the moment when the final letter came through and I knew I was going to Lilleshall as one of the best two goalkeeper in the country for my age group.'

This was the first ever group that The FA brought forward from this system, so it was pretty hard to understate the expectations and pressure upon all those involved to make it a success. On the whole, the group was probably the best 25 in the country at the time, maybe with the exception of a couple of others who chose not to go or didn't make it through the selection for whatever reason. Looking back, though, Tony reminisces on a squad that possibly didn't fulfil its objective of creating full-international players. 'There isn't anyone that I can remember from that squad going on to make a proper international appearance', he says. 'The thing with my group is that we were exposed to an abundance of football, sometimes it was maybe a little too much.'

'In latter years, the ranks have been peppered by the likes

of Jamie Carragher, Sol Campbell and Andy Cole who came through the Lilleshall system, before going on to have very decorated careers including being involved with the England setup, so I certainly don't think it was a long-term problem that Lilleshall faced - just, potentially, a couple of teething problems that needed to be rectified.'

Back at Birmingham, though, and things didn't quite work out so well.

A BOYHOOD DREAM

'It was a real shame for me because my dream was to make a career there and have a proper impact on the club and its history. My debut, especially, was very tough. I didn't know I was playing until a couple of hours before the game, having already been involved with a youth team game that morning, and it also didn't help that the game just happened to be the local derby, against Aston Villa in the Littlewoods Cup, as it was then known.' Martin Thomas was the first-team Birmingham goalkeeper at the time, on loan from Newcastle, and at the last minute Newcastle revoked his ability to play in the game as they didn't want him cup-tied, meaning that Tony received the phone call every goalkeeper dreams about as a youngster... From there, though, it went very sour, very quickly.

'We lost the game 5-0 and I always picked up the blame for that. Whilst the goals weren't my fault, and any goalkeeper would've probably conceded them, I was the one they seemed to scapegoat for the loss. It was supposed to be a special night, full of celebration and promise for the future'. Tony ponders, with a clear underlying sensation of disappointment in his voice, 'but by the end of the 90 minutes, my family were in tears. That sums up the evening pretty well, to be honest. The staff and fans at Birmingham City never really saw that side of it, they had no idea how much it affected me, and, as a youngster, that really hurt'.

There's no doubt that the experience had a long-lasting and profound influence on Tony and it's a shame he looks back on his time with the club he dreamed about with such poor memories. He left the club a few months later, with just the one, fateful, senior appearance. 'I absolutely don't want to darken my love for Birmingham City', Tony says 'but I just don't think that there was an acceptance of myself - or another lad who went to Lilleshall - at the club. It was as though Birmingham saw us as too elite for their setup. They pushed us down the pecking order and didn't look after us in the way that you expect a club to look after its players, at least in comparison to some of our teammates at other clubs.'

It's testament - and not surprising - to Tony's character, however, that he finds at least some silver lining from the ordeal. 'Looking on the positive side, though, the experiences I got from that period at the club have been invaluable. I'd never, ever, treat an individual in the way I was treated for those few months.' Tony takes the opportunity, in this moment, to remind me of the age-old quote that manipulates itself into almost every conversation we hold: 'People will forget what you do or what you say, but they'll always remember how you make them feel'.

Figure 1: Tony (goalkeeper!) and his team, with Brendan as their coach. These early days are part of Tony's inspiration to remain in the game.

Figure 2: Tony (middle) warming up with Mike Kelly and Alan Miller at the Lilleshall National Training Camp. A great experience for Tony to be part of an incredible programme.

Figure 3: Tony (both) in his early days... Little did he know, but Tony was set to be a staunch blue nose, right from the off!

Figure 4: Tony (middle, green) in a squad photo at Birmingham City - his boyhood club.

II
BAPTISM OF FIRE

Next up was Hereford. By self-admission, Tony was struggling with the game that he'd adored since a child. Despite only being in his late teens, he was already starting to consider a career outside of the game. Until he received a call from Ian Bowyer, then manager of Hereford United, that was: 'I'd fallen out of love with the game of football and so was incredibly relieved to be picked up by Ian', who some might say saved Tony's career.

All it took was one short phone call. Ian explained that he had an upcoming friendly that would be a good chance for Tony to showcase himself; a desperate Tony obliged. 'My main thought process, at that point, was probably more "what have I got to lose?" than anything else.'

'I went down to the club, met Ian and the players and most importantly put in a really good performance that I could be proud of. It did have a bit of a training ground game feel to it, but I felt very comfortable, and afterwards Ian invited me into the club on a short-term contract. It was just what I needed in terms of building confidence again, despite the daily drive from Birmingham to Hereford in my dad's car whilst living with my parents!'

'Within a matter of what felt like days, Ian decided he'd seen enough to reward me with my first team debut for the club', retells Tony, excitedly. It was all the more impressive as it was to dislodge Kevin Rose, who had just broken the record for consecutive run of games as goalkeeper for Hereford standing somewhere around the 250 appearance mark.

'The debut was in the Welsh Cup and I was shocked', recalls Tony, as he remembers that he was told he'd be starting on the morning of the game once more. 'Ultimately, it was a huge delivery of trust from Ian and he was saying that he'd successfully done his due diligence and was happy that I was the character and goalkeeper he wanted to take forward for his squad. I was still a youngster at the time, probably just 19 or 20, and my time at Hereford was a rollercoaster of emotions and opportunities from that point onwards.

'I think it was the timing of the move that helped more than anything else', explains Tony, when probed on the reasons why the move was such a saviour. I'd left Birmingham under a bit of a cloud and was in a stage of limbo, to be honest. It was at the point where I was starting to consider packing in football because I'd just had enough. I'd left Lilleshall, an environment where we were encouraged to flourish, to love football and to be the best that we could be and - for one reason or another - there was a huge dichotomy when I returned back at Birmingham'.

BAPTISM OF FIRE

One of the first ways that Tony described his time at Hereford to me was as a 'baptism of fire' - a term that I only started to understand when he recounted some of his most memorable appearances for the Bulls: 'I remember that my Football League debut was at Cambridge United, an away game that we lost 2-1. It was a real eye-opener for me as an 19-year-old, especially as the goalscorer of both Cambridge goals was none other than Dion Dublin! To be thrown in against a player like that, and a manager like John Beck (who was infamous for getting under the skin of the opposition) was a huge learning experience for me and one that really helped to shape the rest of my time with the club.

The second game we discussed, and indeed watched

highlights of in Tony's Eccles home, was the iconic FA Cup match against Sir Alex Ferguson's Manchester United. Following a tough three rounds against clubs such as Merthyr Tydfil, Farnborough and Walsall, Tony tells me about the build up to the draw, as well as the infamous day itself. 'In those days, the draw was completed immediately after the third round games so we all headed upstairs to the bar post-match and huddled around the television. It was about 5:15 on the BBC, and the draw had just begun. A few big clubs had gone by the time that our name came up, but we knew there were still a number of absolute gems left in the bag and that there was always the possibility we could draw one.'

'Suddenly, before the announcer had even presented the name of our opposition, the whole bar jumped to its feet on site of seeing the numbered ball, in raptures of celebration. It absolutely erupted. We knew, at that precise moment, that we had one of - if not the - biggest games of Hereford United's history.'

'The build-up to the game was priceless. It lasted a good two to three weeks. 'We went down to Torquay and did some training on the beach, which was a great way of bonding with the lads in itself. To know that I was going to be pitting my wits against the likes of wonderful players such as Mark Hughes and Viv Anderson was an incredible thought, especially given that Sir Alex was under a little bit of pressure that season. It suggested to us that we had a slight chance.'

The Hereford team were, without a doubt, determined to try and make the most of any inch they were given. 'I didn't have too many saves to make in the game, as it was quite a tight contest. There was an excellent touch round the post in the first half from a deflected Mark Hughes shot, where I've had my bodyweight going one way and had to change direction quickly to get something on the football. Other than that, there wasn't much 'goalkeeping', as such: we had them under control and were applying a bit of pressure ourselves for the majority of the match.'

Things, though, would seem not quite to sway in Tony's direction, as a little piece of trickery and magic would put an end to Hereford's dreams with just minutes to spare: 'It was absolutely gutting when they scored with six or seven minutes left on the clock. I can remember the attack vividly. They broke down the right-hand side, before Mike Duxbury whipped in a cross through the six-yard box and - unfortunately for me - Clayton Blackmore was free at the far post.'

'The Hereford crowd fell silent at that moment and it was such a disappointment.' Still a great achievement, I remind Tony, but his response is probably fitting of the natural dejection that would follow such a knock-out blow. 'I'm proud of how we performed looking back, but in that moment there's a horrible feeling of hollow numbness that you just can't escape from - it doesn't matter if it's Manchester United or a team in the league below us.' An incredibly mature recollection from Tony who would have only been 20 or so at the time, pushed head first into an experience that he will have undoubtedly taken from into the remainder of his career.

INJURY

In a cut-throat career where body parts are at an absolute premium, there is nothing that worries a footballer more than the ever-present risk of picking up an injury that could end a journey before it's even started. As our conversation moves to talk of Tony's career-ending issues, there is a deep and perturbing tension that runs through the air: 'Looking back, it's quite scary. I had ligament damage in my spine, which I got whilst playing for Cardiff City down at Orient', he explains.

It has come to light throughout our interviews that there are many events and turning points in Tony's life that he remembers vividly. I was struck, nonetheless, by the level of depth and detail with which he could recall that fateful day. 'As I struck the ball, my studs got caught in the grass and I've fallen back, almost a whole 90 degrees - the only way I can describe it is like something out of The Matrix. There was also a massive clonk in my pelvic area. Trying to push myself back up from the fall, I realised I couldn't straighten myself up once I'd managed to get to my feet.'

Tony continued ambling around the goalmouth area for the next passage of the game, but the situation worsened when he moved forward to collect a through ball: 'There was an excruciating pain in my back... It was like nothing I've ever felt before. Just raw pain as I tried to come out and claim this ball.' It was at this point that Tony realised he had a serious problem.

'Somehow - and I'm not quite sure how looking back - I managed to get through the rest of the game, avoiding the ball where I could and in absolute agony at the same time.'

'What sticks out most, though, is the coach journey after the match, where I had to lie on the floor at the back of the coach all the way from London to Cardiff, however many miles that journey was. As I got in the car to try and get home, there was an absolute burning sensation through my lower back and buttock, to the point where there was no way I could sit down on it.'

The fast and high-impact nature of football, as well as the naturally congested fixture list, would do Tony no favours, as the team had debatably the biggest derby match of their season (Swansea City) looming around the corner, just three days later. 'The physios injected me, gave me a plethora of painkillers and were basically trying everything and anything that they could to get me through the match of football',

Tony says. 'The pain, though, was unbearable. Coming into the dressing room at half-time, I was trying to explain to the physio that I couldn't continue the game, but all he told me was that I'd be fine and that there was nothing wrong with me.'

This would prove to be the picture with Tony for many months to follow. Despite every attempt from Tony to express his agony and dismay, it often fell upon deaf ears. 'I remonstrated with them quite vigorously, and over time they basically isolated me, just because they couldn't find the issue immediately. For months, I was totally out of the first-team picture, training with the youngsters and away from the day-to-day happenings of the club.'

'Over this period of time I'd had just about every injection, x-ray or scan that you could imagine.' As Tony speaks, now, his frustration and helplessness towards the situation is palpable. 'Literally, there was no stone left unturned - from radiation scans, to acupuncture, to having my facet joints injected with a needle that was about 10 or 11 inches long.'

Still, though, there was an heir of suspicion around Tony and his 'phantom' injury. 'People didn't seem to understand, to a degree, that I wasn't just going to put myself through this ordeal for nothing. I had a major problem that was having a severe effect on my life.'

'I'd given up on the staff at Cardiff and was really frustrated with the whole situation, before it was actually my local GP who had the breakthrough. It turns out that my GP had seen similar cases with these kinds of symptoms in various rugby players, so he gave me a steroid injection and we monitored the situation over the next few weeks. We knew that, if I felt relief over this time period, something had to be working and, lo and behold, over the next three weeks I started to feel a little less pain and got that invaluable relief that I had been starved of for so long.'

'Because of the success the medication had found, the doctor decided that it was appropriate to inject me with a sclerosing agent. The only way I can really describe it is that it forms a bond at the end of the torn ligaments, bringing them back together artificially', Tony says, as I ask him in a little more detail how the agent works. 'What we have to understand is that our ligaments are like chewing gum: very pliable and very stretchy.'

'The sclerosing agent, though, is not pliable - it's as if you've taken the chewing gum and left it in the freezer. Whilst it might last forever and be a really effective piece of artificial kit, the danger was that - under the right (or wrong!) circumstances - it might just pull apart, and you wouldn't be able to form them together again after that: it would be game over.'

And that, for Tony, would seem to be the perfect solution to the problem that had destroyed so much of his life over the previous year. He found himself quickly moved on from Cardiff, but back in the game - nonetheless - with a great chance to prove himself once more. 'I'd moved away from Cardiff at the time, as they'd brought another goalkeeper in, but a manager I'd worked with before (Mick Wadsworth) took me to Scarborough once I was fit again', recalls Tony. 'I went up for their play-off campaign, having a really good three or four months with them.' It wouldn't take too long, though, for Tony's worst nightmare to bubble above the surface once more.

In a game at home to Darlington, with the balance of play on a knife edge and just before the half-time whistle, lightning struck for the second time: 'I innocuously went up for a cross, back-pedalling slightly as I took the ball and fell backwards. All I heard was a strange, abstract 'clonk' noise in my back. The feeling was identical: there was no doubt about what I had done.'

'Tracy was in the crowd watching, knowing the pain I was in and I can't imagine what she must have been going through. I signalled to the medical staff that I had a pretty huge problem, but still - when I went in at half-time - they were determined for me to play the second-half. Hobbling, limping and very much struggling to have any real impact on the game, I played through the second-half, which would prove to be my last 45 minutes of football'.

When asked whether Tony was aware that there was no

coming back second time around, he stopped talking for a moment. 'Yes', he eventually murmured. 'I knew at that point that it was game over'.

Figure 5: Tony holding the Welsh Cup that he won with Hereford during his early years in the professional game.

Figure 6: Tony in a rather retro goalkeeper kit at Cardiff City - the club where he would go on to suffer his career-limiting injury.

Figure 7: Tony (both) in his early days... Little did he know, but Tony was set to be a staunch blue nose, right from the off!

Figure 8: Tony at his final club, Scarborough, and in his final push before injury would strike again.

III

DEFINING MOMENTS

Speak to any former-professional footballer and they'll tell you about the difficulty in coming down from the extreme emotions, intensities and ecstasies of football back into the harsh reality of the 'real' world. What they may not tell you, though, is how that drop is amplified for those who end the game before their peak, whilst still mentally at the top, through career-ending injuries such as Tony's. The journey from this point on was always set to be a rocky road for Tony, but one that he faced up to and tackled with that grit and determination that seems to underline his persona.

'I went to see a surgeon and had a variety of scans, again, but the overall verdict was that there was nothing we could do to repair any damage; the best, or only, solution was to stop playing. I was still in pain for the next 12 months or so with a lot of numbness in my left leg. You have to appreciate that, as an elite athlete, there's a level of physical capacity that you have to be capable of working at and I was nowhere near it during that period.'

'Over the years, the pain has eased and I've started to find ways to work around the issues. It's a bit of a nuisance, but it doesn't affect my work, which is one of the issues we could've had. Having had discussions with the surgeon, had I continued to try and play through the pain barrier, there's a real potential that I'd be sat here in a wheelchair right now, certainly not having had the coaching career I've created for myself.'

'The fact it was a back injury was really worrying, and I certainly had to be very careful because of that. It was a tough time, for sure: pensions were small back in those days, wages were generally lower and there just weren't so many opportunities for footballers to move into other, transferable, careers. After a 14 year journey, I ended up leaving the game with about £30,000. That was everything I had. It meant we had to move back to Carlisle and live in a council house, living off my pension for the period that I couldn't work because of my back. We certainly had to be very humble and learn to deal with the situation: I'm absolutely of the notion that it has helped to transform me into the coach and person I am today, there's no doubt about that.'

As soon as Tony could physically get himself back to work, he found a night-shift at the local Morrisons. 'It was different, exhausting and very hard work', he remembers. 'But I managed to battle through it in order to earn a crust and provide some cash for my wife and my kids.'

'It got us through a period after the pension had run out where we just didn't have any money. It was a real reality check, with a very young family that have just moved from a lovely house with no financial concerns what-so-ever, to literally scraping for every pound we could find.'

CARLISLE UNITED

Being out of the game was a tough time for Tony, but there was a very thin line between balancing the requirements and needs of his young family and following his passion to carve a career back in the game. It's no surprise to Tony, or to anyone around him, that this opportunity would prove to be through a coaching capacity.

'Whilst I was working at Morrisons, I also went into doing a bit of goalkeeper work at Workington Reds (which transpired to be more of an assistant coaching role, alongside the then manager Peter Hampton). I was only there for a couple of years first time around, but it really helped to improve my understanding of the game and get a feeling for what playing was like from a coach's perspective. Five or six months later, Tracy and I sat down and had a very honest conversation about what we could do to make ends meet.'

'We were in Carlisle already, and I had a good reputation down at the club because of the career I'd had there, so I thought that if there was any way I'd make a full-time move into the coaching world it would be with them, first and foremost. It might have been a case of being patient for a while, waiting for the opportunity to present itself, but it turned out to be an excellent decision, working out brilliantly in the latter years.

The building blocks would take a large deal of grafting for Tony, but the resilience from his career would ultimately take him to a point where he'd reached that goal of working for Carlisle. 'Whilst I was at Workington, I actually set up my own private goalkeeping schools, which was really starting to get me noticed and build up a reputation for my work as a youth developer within the grassroots game.'

'I plugged away with this for a period of time, helping goalkeepers to develop themselves across a multitude of different facets, whilst enhancing my experience and contact list at every opportunity.'

Taking his work to Carlisle, though, would always be a difficult task. 'The situation politically at Carlisle was a bit messy, with attempted takeovers and proposed chairmen from the left, right and centre, which made it a really tricky situation to try and get in touch with the club.' Tony's saving grace would be Roddy Collins, the infamous manager who had married into the Elliott family. 'All of a sudden, I was involved in the picture as there was a suggestions that Roddy Collins may be coming in as manager. It was heavily likely that he may want me to be his goalkeeper coach.'

'Within days of him being awarded the job, I got a phone call and was invited in to the training ground for a chat. It didn't take much conversing before he offered me the job and I was first-team goalkeeper coach at Carlisle!'

It may sound like a whirlwind from the outside, but that isn't half of the hectic storm that preceded - and proceeded - Tony's appointment at the club. 'It was quite a difficult period at times, as the takeover was in a messy situation and there was a huge squabble to try and wrestle the club away from its previous owners. There was certainly a lot of talk around the town as to what may be going on, but no-one on beyond the club really understood the full extent of the issues.'

Just as everything appeared as though it may be settling down and the buyout was on the table, disaster struck once more. 'I remember being told that the buyout had fallen through, and therefore that we'd been relieved of our positions and Roddy Collins was sacked.' After two months of thumb-twiddling and staring at walls, the buyout and takeover was officially confirmed, with Tony and Roddy being reinstated, and the new chairman sending all of the backroom staff onto the pitch to be welcomed by the fans once more.

'I think I was more relieved than anything else, if I'm honest, because it'd been such a roller-coaster journey for the club. It was great to see everything appear a little more stable again'. A positive couple of seasons followed for Tony, before Roddy lost his job, with Tony leaving the club with him to return to his goalkeeping schools.

DEFINING MOMENTS

The hard work and dedication towards these centres moved to a whole new level, when one of Tony's very talented young goalkeepers, who'd been with him for a couple of years, was playing a county representative game.

'There were two scouts at the game that day: one from Liverpool and one from Manchester United. The 'keeper had an absolutely fantastic game, showcasing everything he had to offer, and both clubs contacted his parents to invite him down to their training complexes for trials. The question both clubs asked to the parents, without fail, was "who has your son been working with?".'

'Of course, at this point, my name was thrown onto the table', recalls Tony, 'and within 48 hours I had contact from both clubs asking me to setup what transpired to be the latest movement in the academy game: goalkeeping development centres for outside the club's catchment area, so that goalkeepers could be improved and identified before being moved on to the academy.'

Tony couldn't turn down an incredible opportunity to produce goalkeepers on their way to the elite level, but he had a complication on his hand with two of the biggest clubs in England - if not the world - arguing over his signature. 'In the end, a cocktail of gut instinct and intuition led me to choosing Liverpool.' We set up one centre in Preston and our aim for that was to establish one goalkeeper that was good enough to be looked at by the academy within the first three years.'

'That target was absolutely smashed, having three goalkeepers actually go on to physically sign for the academy in the first year alone. Whether it was by luck or by judgement I'm not sure, but it was decided that someone else should run the development centres, with me moving into a more integrated role with the academy, coming in one or two times a week to do work with the academy goalkeepers.'

Over time, Tony's role within the setup expanded further, and he started to take a more supervisory role over the leading of international soccer camps in addition to his academy work.

After Rafa Benitez left, though, there was a realisation among all the staff members that the academy setup was going to be changing, to suit the new manager coming in, so Tony decided then that it was time to be on the look for a new pathway: a new environment to set himself up in and continue to grow.

Again, things seemed to settle into place quite well for Tony, as the head of goalkeeping at Manchester City (Roy Tucks) happened to partner him as a tutor for an FA Level 1 Goalkeeper Course, delivering to a number of new goalkeeper coaches. 'We spent three days together getting to know each other a little better. The end product of it was that I walked out with a new job... I got a phone call about a week later from Roy, the tutor, asking how I was getting on and what my plans were, and then he went on to tell me that he really enjoyed the course we delivered together and that, actually, he wanted me to go and work for him at Manchester City.'

At first, Tony was pretty taken aback, because it was very unexpected. He rapidly realised, however, that Manchester City were becoming one of the biggest clubs in the world, with all the money and resources being pumped into them. 'This was a fantastic chance for me to propel myself within the footballing world', Tony told me.

'I went and met Roy, we had a chat, and in the back of my

mind was always that I wanted to get out of Liverpool whilst everything was still good. We managed to reach an agreement for me to go and do some work for Manchester City, with a very similar arrangement to that at Liverpool (in the sense of setting up development structures) but I only really had time to put the framework and structure in place for this, before my work with The FA snowballed and I found myself immersed with the new futsal programme.'

FUTSAL

Tony's first adventure outside the mainstream format of the game was one that opened his mind - and career - to a multitude of different learning opportunities, chances for reflection and tools that would go on to create the multi-faceted coach that he is today. If it wasn't for the actions of a couple of influential characters, though, Tony may not have had the same opportunity to build an affinity with football's indoor, technically-based and intense counterpart.

'Interestingly, the main reason that the futsal opportunity came about was because of the work I had been doing at Liverpool and the contacts that had been built up. Graeme Dell, the England futsal coach at the time, was looking for a new goalkeeper coach, and contacted the head of goalkeeping at Liverpool, Billy Stewart, asking if he wanted the job. Billy replied with something along the lines of "I can't, and my assistant Tim Dittmer can't, but we've got a guy called Tony Elliott, who could well be interested in the position". So Delly got in contact with me, inviting me down to Lilleshall the following weekend to have a look around at the sport, the facilities, and also to do a little bit of work with the goalkeepers.'

'As soon as I arrived, I realised there was something pretty special about the sport and by the end of the day I had been totally mesmerised by it: I was in love with the game of futsal. My mind was racing during the journey home, and as soon as Delly contacted me to say that he was happy with my work and wanted to offer me the job I bit his hand off and said I'd be delighted to join the team!' The rest, you might say, is history...

Tony's journeys with the squad have been far- and wide-reaching. They've experienced a lot of turbulence along the way, but the beauty of the growth within the sport is that there are always clearer skies to look forward to, with more opportunities to build exceptional teams that can compete in top-level competition. The clear skies have, without a doubt, already started to reveal themselves.

'With the futsal squad, we've had the pleasure of travelling the globe to compete in a number of world and European qualifying competitions'. Tony tells me that he has around 80 'appearances' as a coach for the senior futsal squad, and these have spanned a number of different competitions and events.

'As a squad, we always had to pre-qualify for the major tournaments because of where futsal has come from in this country and the lack of reputation that it has. It's still very much in its infancy, but five, even 10 years ago, it really was at the most basic level you can imagine for such a popular game world-wide.'

That didn't stop Tony and his team pushing the existing boundaries, though, as they sought the opportunity to prove themselves on the main stage. 'About three or four years ago we went to Lithuania in the World Championship pre-qualifiers. Matched in a group with Lithuania and Cyprus, it was always going to be the best chance we ever had of qualifying to get through to the elite stages and playing some of the big teams.'

EUPHORIA

'Our first game was against Lithuania, in an incredibly hostile stadium where the fans were nearly on top of us and all 1500 of them baying for English blood.' Tony, now, has a rather excited tone to his voice and that look in his eye that only comes from experiencing a victory against the odds.

'It was an unbelievable game. We were winning relatively comfortably, before having a man sent off and being forced a man down. The rules in futsal dictate that you can't then replace that player until either two minutes has passed, or the opposition manage to score a goal. We were defending for our lives at this point and there were only a couple of minutes on the clock. I remember that we had been absolutely bombarded by the Lithuanians throughout the period, and felt a huge sense of relief when our fifth player ran back on to the pitch to return us to full compliment.'

'All of a sudden, though, the referee blew his whistle and sent the player that had just come on back off the pitch: he had ran on a second before the two minutes was up, therefore seeing another red card and forcing us to play the last minute and 45 seconds with three outfield players.'

'It was absolutely frantic', says Tony. 'The raucous Lithuanian crowd did nothing to dampen the tension and Tony can barely remember the number of blocks, saves and all-round defensive heroics during what must have been 100 seconds, max. Somehow, and it really was 'somehow', we managed to win the game, not conceding again, and the euphoria we felt was absolutely incredible.'

The Lithuanian crowd had been silenced and the team were zealous with enthusiasm and joy, after managing to see out a game that most would have looked at and simply marked impossible. Looking back on the photos of the game, it's clear to me just how much that meant to Tony and his team. It was real, tangible, raw emotion at its very finest. If people want to talk about passion, drive and determination, these pictures sum it up in an absolute nutshell.

Very quickly, though, Tony and his team turned their attention to Cyprus, knowing that another similar performance would be required in order to see the team compete in the main qualifying event. 'We knew going into that game that if we could win it, we'd be guaranteed to be through for the first time in English futsal history.'

'There was no consideration for trying to draw the game, we went out with the sole motion of attacking and being positive. On the day, I think we had a little bit too much about us for Cyprus and that's what helped us to get over the line. We went 2-0 up, and then they scored to put it back to 2-1. As the clock continued to tick from thirty seconds, to twenty seconds, we were an absolute wreck on the sideline waiting for the final buzzer. The sound of relief echoed through the stadium and I literally fell to my knees.'

'The players were going mental all around us but I was down on the floor through exhaustion and passion for what we'd done - the heights we'd reached had never been achieved before. The goalkeepers came over to me and helped me off the floor, before we just hugged each other for one or two minutes and then joined the rest of the team.'

'There were tears, everywhere, it was just such an incredible experience and it brings back really raw and momentous emotions looking back. It was an absolutely euphoric feeling because we were the first squad ever to achieve this with futsal in England, and I suppose it helped to put into perspective some of the thrashings that we'd had back in the early 2000s, at the start of the programme. They make you question why you're in the game and investing so much time into trying to succeed.'

'The feelings we had after the Cyprus game brought everything home and gave me a real sense of purpose. If I look back over my life experiences, there's probably nothing that I value higher than that moment, with the exception of the birth of my children and marriage with Tracy. It gives me chills down my spine even thinking about it now, because it's the first time in my footballing career that I've actually cried. I broke down inside the stadium and I can clearly remember the feelings of how incredible it seemed to be the first England futsal team to break through the pre-qualifying stage. We would have the opportunity to compete with elite-level futsal players at a higher level for the first time: it was sheer euphoria; an absolute high of my coaching career.'

Linking in once more with one of our future areas for discussion, there's no doubt in Tony's mind that it was the sacrifice of the players that allowed them to reach this euphoria, and that they fully deserved it because of that.

'These boys had given up so much in terms of effort, finances, and unrelenting commitment to the programme that it was incredible to see it all pay off, and for them to finally have the opportunity to compete at that elite level'.

In the eyes of many around football, though, that achievement wasn't quite replicated when they returned to home soil. 'The journey home was a bit strange, really - almost anticlimactic in a way. If this had been the senior football squad, there would've been press officers, journalists and photographers piled through the airport on our return, all wanting a little piece of the incredible story that had seen us qualify, so that they could take it to the back pages of the major papers the next day. For us, though, nobody knew.'

'It was very insular to the futsal family, and maybe it's a shame that nobody knew just how big what we achieved was: this was an absolute breakthrough moment for English futsal that wasn't celebrated anywhere near enough. There was so much more that could have been done with that momentous tournament, but I guess that's where we need to see the improvement in the infrastructure and resources that English futsal benefits from at present.'

RIO 2016

Looking at Tony's disability perspective on the game,

we've spoken on many occasions about the difference between the domestic and the international setup during his time as a coach. Not just in the sake of interviews for this book, but also on a much broader spectrum of conversation. There's one message and idea that has reverberated around Tony's position, which seems to become clearer and clearer with everything he says. 'To me, being an international coach is everything. I'll sit here when I've got time off in my GB tracksuit, it's just how I relax.'

'It's not because I'm ego-driven or want everyone to see all the incredible projects I've been involved in, it's because I love the work that I do with the national squads and it means so, so much to me. That's always been the way I've felt about the three lions and the opportunity and honour to play and coach my country.

And it was this zest for coaching and representing international players that saw Tony pick up his position within the Cerebral Palsy game, which would ultimately take him to the pinnacle of any disabled athlete's career: the Paralympics.

'My experiences with the Cerebral Palsy squad have been far-reaching, ever since I took over after London 2012, with a number of competitions across Europe - including the World Championships - and obviously culminating with Rio this summer just gone. Anyone involved with the setup will openly agree that Keith and I took the team and group on to massively greater things. They're probably realised as the third or fourth best teams in the world now'.

'It's interesting, because you're one of the first people I've had the conversation with about Rio. You're one of the first to really want to understand what it was about and quite how much of an achievement it was for us as a squad. To a degree, that's been a bit of a disappointment for me', explains Tony, reservedly.

'There was probably a bit of a stigma attached to it because of the Paralympics and people not believing it transfers well to other formats of the game, but no-one's really wanted to learn from the experience. No one has had a huge desire to speak with me and reflect about how things went, how things could be improved in the future and ultimately how to become a better coach because of it. The fact it was GB and not England might have made a difference, but that really shouldn't matter: the England staff are the GB staff and so the two programmes are very closely linked, if not the same thing in reality - we had three Scottish players in our team but the other ten were English.'

As we discussed the relationship between Tony and his members of staff in more detail, there was one individual who Tony thought particularly fondly of during his time with the programme. 'Keith [Webb] and I have a great relationship, having worked together for four years now and constantly bounced ideas off one another during that time. What I love about the way we work is that we're both very open about the other's knowledge, experience and ideas: I'm more than happy for Keith to share any piece of information he might have to the players and I'm sure he'd reciprocate that trust and understanding.'

Moving on to the tournament, Tony and his team always knew it was going to be difficult as they had the hosts - Brazil - in their group, as well as Ukraine, who were one of the other big teams in the competition and would prove a real test for the GB side. 'We had the team in a fantastic position, with a solid plan, but ultimately we were undone by having the two favourites for the competition in our group, as a result of Russia being banned from the tournament late on. We couldn't have asked any more from the boys, taking both teams very close - we only lost to Ukraine through a penalty. I truly believed that we scared them during that tournament, they hated playing us and our style of play really disturbed them.'

This wasn't the first encounter between the two, though. 'If we go back to the European Championships two years ago, we came across Ukraine again. Because they're such a great side (the best in Europe at the time), the expectation is that they'll just destroy you. No one expected a contest from the game at all. Having said that, Keith and I sat down before that tournament and asked ourselves what we could do to disrupt this thinking pattern. We knew that we had players who could create something on the ball, but the most important thing was to stop them scoring. We brainstormed, considered and debated, before deciding on a system we knew would break them down and prevent them from being able to score in the ways they had done previously.'

As seems to have been a commonly reverberating theme within the Cerebral Palsy squad, it very nearly paid off for Tony's side. 'We were 1-0 up with less than two minutes to go against the favourites for the tournaments, when Ukraine managed to put the ball in the net and draw the game with us. It might have been a bit of a disappointment in the moment, but on reflection it created an absolute shockwave across CP football. Ultimately, Keith and I had created this 3-3 system that worked so effectively in frustrating the opposition.' When we discuss aspects later on in the book such as the goalkeeper coach's role in providing support and advice across the coaching staff, this example of how Tony had worked and collaborated almost fully in tandem with his over-arching manager is a great example of how the goalkeeper coach can impact the larger team surroundings, with great success for all involved.

Moving back to Rio, and Tony faced a similar situation where it would take something innovative and bold to see the team progress in the competition. 'We couldn't use the same system against the Ukrainians again, of course, as they knew what to expect, so we sat the players down and asked them something along the lines of "do you want to come here and play it safe, staying defensive but probably being broken down over the course of the game, or do you want to really frighten these teams and have a real go at giving them a great match?". The answer was a resounding attraction towards the second idea, with every one of the players in the room chomping at the bit to get started and push the boundaries of what exactly was possible. It was all Keith and I needed to hear.'

'We set ourselves up to defend and protect the middle', which was only possible for Tony's team because of the amount of time that they had to discuss defensive detail over a variety of media. 'As a coach, it's taught me that using the different media we have at our disposal is vital to success.'

'If you've got the knowledge of different formats, philosophies and ideologies on how the game of football should be played, in whatever format, there will always be opportunities to share and transfer them; the key element is recognising the right moment and when you're best to just sit on something for a little while.

'History will show that we lost both games 2-1', says Tony, 'but what it won't show is quite how close the margins were in both games and the statement that this made.'

I ask Tony, also, if he is disappointed with the finishing

position of the side (5th) and the fact that they didn't have the opportunity to play in a medal match. 'I'm not disappointed about the tournament for a second', Tony replies without hesitation. 'I'm just so proud of being part of a great unit and an incredible group of people, who took two of the best teams in the world all the way and nearly beat them in the end. There are an abundance of learnings that I can take from the experience as a coach, from the analysis that we undertook, to the preparation and planning that Keith and I relentlessly toiled with, even to the extent where we starting to tap into my futsal brain and philosophies for the Ukraine game, just to give us that edge and try something different.'

Having an understanding of how you can use skill-sets from different formats to create a more resourceful and detailed goalkeeper that can pull on different techniques due to the context of the moment is imperative. Tony likes to use the analogy of a golfer.

'If you travel around a golf course, with a putter and a wood, what kind of round are you going to have? It's going to be very tough, and at times you're going to have to play shots that you just know you can't play, winging it a little bit. Consider, on the other hand, that you've got 10 or 12 clubs, all suited for different conditions and contexts. You're going to have a much better chance of playing a good round and ultimately achieving a much improved end-product'.

'You still, though, have to be able to swing those clubs?', I responded.

'Yes, of course: as the saying goes, you can take a horse to water, but you can't make it drink. I can give them the clubs and the tools that they might need to succeed, but, ultimately, when they choose to use them is a decision for my goalkeepers to make.'

It's clear to Tony that this must be a player-led process, and that the player must use a great deal of ownership and autonomy over the decisions they make. 'We can use imagery, analysis, feedback or any other aids you can come up with, but when the players step on to the pitch, the decisions they make and the tools they feel are most appropriate are totally on their own backs. That's the way I look at things: it's all about trying to give people a greater quantity and quality of clubs in the bag.'

And on that first piece of Tony's real practical insight into the world of coaching, we move forward into looking a little deeper at the relationship between player and coach. Indeed, the tools in the coach's bag play a great part in forging and enhancing these connections, in every context.

Figure 9: Tony (middle) with his Carlisle goalkeeper schools - an opportunity to inspire his youth development.

Figure 10: Tony (middle) with futsal goalkeepers Tom Dennis and Dylan Malpas.

Figure 11: Tony (first light blue) and the futsal staff proudly singing the national anthem pre-competition.

Figure 12: Tony (far left) with the futsal squad, after their triumph in Lithuania.

Figure 13: Tony (second right) and the blind squad taking silver at the Seoul World Games - see more on this story from Dan James in the 'Case Study' section.

Figure 14: Tony (third right, back row) with the Cerebral Palsy squad on their way to Rio 2016.

Figure 15: Does this photo need a description? Tony before his first game in Rio!

Figure 16: Tony (middle) with Giles and Ryan, the two CP goalkeepers, inside the Rio stadium.

Section Two

Developing the person

IV
RESPECT

Writing this element of the book has been, without a doubt, one of the most insightful, reflective and fascinating passages of the project. Tony's abundant philosophies of sharing, caring and learning underlined every one of our conversations to produce thoughts and perspectives that are as relevant for everyday life as they are for goalkeeping-specific coaches.

A lifetime in the game brings around many opportunities for self-awareness, reflection and conscious feeling, as long as the participant is open-minded to learning through sport and the lessons that it can bring. Not only have Tony's highs and lows shaped this ideology within his life, but they have also kindled his desire to share them with fellow coaches.

Starting with respect, and moving through into aspects such as intuition, passion and connection, each facet of Tony's character - and leadership ability - is a huge pillar in building strong and purposeful relationships with those he comes across, in order to help them improve themselves. It is, if you like, the hidden art of coaching, and one that not many people conquer quite like Tony.

'Respect, for me, is a two-way process', says Tony. 'It's not just in football or sport that respect is an important facet: it's a vital cog in the way in which the human world functions.' As an underpinning factor of Tony's behaviour as a coach, he also realises that this two-way process can sometimes be lost by those who lack self-awareness.

'We become far too attached to ourselves sometimes, forgetting that other people matter as well and sometimes it's helpful to just step back, assess a situation and have the respect to understand how other people might be feeling as a result of your actions.'

'Across all the formats I've worked in, it's patently obvious that each has a differing set of dynamics and trends that I've got to adjust to, but every time that I've walked through that door, I've had the utmost respect for the people I'm about to meet and collaborate with.'

BACKGROUNDS

'We've all got a different story, coming from a multitude of backgrounds with an abundance of experiences earlier in our lives, regardless of whether we're international goalkeepers or just playing for our Sunday League team at the weekend', Tony explains, as he makes reference to the fact that it's not always easy to empathise with the position that others are in. 'We've got to appreciate what daily life is like for everyone and that we don't always understand the challenges that people face, even as coaches who build a relationship with their players.'

'There are a variety of different ways in which I show players that I have respect for them. You have to give them the right to share their opinions and show their feelings and thoughts. This can be hard at times if it's something you don't agree with, but ultimately it's recognising how people want to be treated and what makes them tick.'

Of course, this changes considerably for Tony depending on the environment in which he is working, and sometimes the ideas from one environment will influence attitudes towards another. 'When I took the disability role, it really helped me realise that football isn't just about producing better elite athletes or Premier League stars, it's about creating better lives. That joy, that connection, that happiness that you bring to somebody else is what football comes down to, very simply.'

'In order to recognise this, and put the person above the player, you have to have an incredible amount of respect for the people you're working with. If Tony is to summarise how he would define the importance of respect, then: 'it's all about asking yourself how you can make their story and ultimately their experiences in this life that little bit better and a bit more fulfilling.'

IDEOLOGIES

As Tony and I continue to discuss the topic of respect, we start to move away from the traditional sense of coach-player relationships, but also talk about respect for the 'job', if you like, and the different ideologies within coaching.

'Sometimes it can be about respecting the different processes that work, as well as the people. Everyone has their own way of working, and sometimes we can get caught up in our own philosophies and believing that there's only one correct way to produce an outcome. Approaching situations with an open-mind is incredibly important and is born, fundamentally, out of a great dose of respect for the systems we use and the ideas of other people.'

'There's always going to be ego between coaches, as we all have different beliefs, feelings and ideas of what is the best way to produce outcomes within groups of footballers. Some coaches are more locked into these philosophies than others, and less comfortable thinking and working outside of their own environments.'

I ask Tony, at this point, what he believes is the ideal compromise between being stubborn towards your beliefs and being influenced by anything and everything that you hear. 'Yes: have an opinion on something, that's very, very important, but also don't be afraid to listen to the opinion of others and let it influence the way you work. It's also about how we share our opinion and whether we use it to empower others as another tool, or to berate and demean them, which is likely to have a very different end result and is a huge sign of disrespect. It's something very wrong for me.'

The ability of coaches to respect each other can also pay dividends in development and collaboration terms, and Tony is very keen to talk about some of his experiences in this regard. 'I've had so many respectful relationships where there've been countless opportunities to share opinions. One of the most rewarding things for a coach is when somebody (especially who maybe initially seemed sceptical of ideas) turns around and says "I like that, it's a good idea and could be of great use to me as I try to take this bunch of individuals forward". That's when you know that somebody does have respect for you, ultimate respect, and is more than likely a result of the way in which you've treated them in the past and how you've made them feel.'

GIVE IT TO GET IT

Moving forward, I question Tony as to how this respect can be obtained for new coaches. 'You certainly have to give it to get it', Tony makes clear, 'and the coach has to take the first step in this relationship as well. They're likely to be the more mature character, and it's up to them to have the impetus to reach out a hand and offer to make individuals feel that bit more important, whilst trying to get an understanding of what life is like in their shoes at the same time. I'm more than happy to give up time in working out what makes a person tick and where that drive comes from.'

The bottom line is, though, that if Tony respects somebody and gives them his time and attention, he absolutely expects that to be reciprocated in the way they treat and buy into his processes.

'Generally, people are clever enough and mature enough to understand the value in a two-way relationship. However, there can be times where the extra freedom and trust that you instil in individuals comes back to bite you, as they choose to use your connection for their own betterment. It's a shame when you're exploited like that, and as a coach you do spend a bit of time reflecting and contemplating about how the situation arose. Personally, though, the most important thing for me is that I've given that individual an opportunity to prove themselves. You can't legislate against that kind of abuse and it's in such a minority that it leaves no dent in my philosophies and how I try to build respectful connections with players.'

I ask Tony if disrespect with previous coaches, or a reputation for a bad attitude can influence his approach and methodologies when working respectfully with an athlete. 'As a coach, I give anyone I work with a clean slate: it's for me to make a judgement about their strengths and shortcomings in character, taking people at face value and giving them an opportunity to show me what they've got to offer before I decide if things are going to work out or not. I believe it can be a little bit dangerous to enter a situation with prejudiced or pre-conceived ideas, because you've got no idea of the circumstances in which those were formed. It's just the way I work, I don't think there's any changing that.'

There's no doubt that respect plays a crucial part in the creation of a successful, autonomous learning environment for Tony and his athletes, and an analogy that he uses, combining the complexity of humans with the dynamism of the game, encapsulates this as an excellent conclusion:

'If we want to create robots, who can't feel or give respect, we're going to produce robotic athletes and robotic outcomes, that aren't fit for the dynamic game we play where respect for a multitude of different situations and contexts is imperative. For me, it's about the difference in life and people; the respect element is one of the pathways through which we achieve that.'

V

OWNERSHIP

A second fundamental pillar in building relationships with his athletes and performers, giving ownership to those who work with Tony is crucial to his philosophies and development outcomes.

There is reason to this, it would seem, both from a psychological and technical perspective. Tony's role is to build goalkeepers with the skills, independence and decision-making abilities to make split-second decisions at the elite reaches of the game, and, without allowing them to take a deal of autonomy over their own development, this would simply not be possible.

Tony and I spoke at some detail around the shifts within the modern game to a player-centred approach and what this means for the goalkeeper coach moving forward.

'Football in the 21st century is certainly more player-driven and the modern coach has a lot of overlaps in the way they work - they're expected to throw a lot of different methods at the players.'

FOUNTAIN OF EXPERTISE

On the role of the coach, Tony is convinced still that coaches have an immense level of support to offer. 'Sometimes we forget, though, that coaches aren't just facilitators of learning; they are one avenue or fountain of expertise, knowledge and experience that their players should be absolutely striving to utilise. We haven't just been handed the piece of paper that says UEFA A, or whatever it might be; an awful lot of work has gone in behind-the-scenes and everyone must appreciate the processes involved to obtain that piece of paper.'

'It's without a doubt that coaches have to drip-feed this fountain of information, though, at the right time for an individual player, or goalkeeper. Sometimes, it might be a case of allowing the players to work the answer out for themselves, even if you're bursting to tell them how they could improve.'

Tony's reasoning behind this is as much practical as it is performance-related.

'Especially when I was involved with the cerebral palsy and blind squads, there were the occasional camps or games that I would miss, as there were calendar clashes with other programmes that I was a part of. During these times, it was imperative that the goalkeepers had the confidence and independence to be able to manage their own warm-up, preparation for the game and solve problems in the moment. Of course, there was a member of support staff to assist them in their preparation, but if all they'd done was absorb information from me over the past 12 months, they wouldn't have been able to cope when they were exposed without a specialist coach to hand.'

The other reason, Tony adds, is from a skill acquisition perspective. 'If we want our goalkeepers to really accelerate and solidify their learning process, then hitting the ball into their metaphorical court is a great way to do that. Their body and, most importantly, decision-making processes will adapt to the stresses they're put under when we force them to create their own solution, which will ultimately produce a self-fulfilling goalkeeper who is able to work effectively both in and away from camp. It's vital when we've only got a few weekends a year working with the players.'

My next question for Tony is around the ways in which he

gives his goalkeepers the autonomy to become independent in the way that they play. 'Sometimes, it can be as simple as involving them in the decision-making process. They know their bodies and their weaknesses better than anything else, so I always make sure I drop them a phone call a couple of days before camp to see what they'd like to work on, and I can then prepare my session around that. It's two-fold, really: as they have a chance to be involved with the decision-making and yet we can be very confident that the session I'm putting on will support their development where they need it most.'

QUESTIONING AND PROBING

'Beyond that, it's largely a case of questioning and probing the goalkeeper over their analysis. It's not my job to point out a list of a thousand mistakes they've made every game, but it might be that I can facilitate their recognition of two or three that we can push forward with in the future.' I ask Tony, also, if his culture of review and reflection supports this. 'Absolutely. That period of reflection for a goalkeeper will be one of the biggest in terms of their ability to take some ownership of their performance and generate their own ideas about how they'd like to improve next time; the onus is on the coach, in my opinion, to give the players this opportunity to reflect - they'll soon be standing on their own two feet!'

One final way in which Tony prompts independence in decision-making is the way in which he delivers some of his sessions. 'I feel as though goalkeepers respond when you force them to figure things out for themselves. In order to create this opportunity, it might be that I have to execute a very high-information exercise, but without giving the goalkeeper too much guidance as to how to deal with it. We might come back and question at points of the training, or I may guide the goalkeeper towards certain conclusions, but the reality is that I'll give them as much time as possible to solve the situations themselves.'

'After all, that's the situation they're going to find themselves in a match at some point during their career, is it not?'

VI
CONNECTION

Almost anybody who knows Tony, and especially those who have experienced him as a mentor or tutor, will know that there are a couple underpinning factors that mould him into the coach he is today. Having struggled through dark and difficult days as both a player and a coach, one of Tony's biggest inspirations is looking up to those who pulled him through his turbulent times, and the connections they forged together. As an international coach, Tony is always eager to further the connection with his goalkeepers, viewing it as one of the fundamental metrics of their success.

IMPERATIVE ROLE

'It's not a case of being egotistical or big-headed, because that will lose you relationships in the long run, but I sincerely believe that I, as a coach, play an imperative role in the connection with my goalkeepers.' Over time, Tony has undoubtedly built up a love of people and sees this as a further mechanism for growing his relationships. 'If there's something that I've started to understand lately, it's that how you are loved, not how you love, that really defines you're ability to connect with an individual. That perception that your goalkeepers, support staff and colleagues have of you when their backs are turned, and the door is closed, is a real signal for me of the strength of relationship that has been built over time.'

My interactions with Tony over the past year would undoubtedly support this idea, having seen first-hand through interviews, conversations and observations the affection that many hold towards Tony and his work. 'People want to spend time with me, they want to share my knowledge and they're interested in what I have to say'.

When asked why he believes this is, the answer is simple. 'I can connect with people', replies Tony, clicking his fingers, 'that's just me.'

However, this ability to connect with those working

around him is not an overnight accomplishment, but instead the result of hours of work, trial and error, and building a set of qualities that will support his relationships with others. Passion, therefore, must be at the heart of it. 'Football, or futsal, is my route to share experience, knowledge and leave a legacy. All I ever want is that, when I'm gone, people remember me and love me for what I've done in the game. Everything I do is geared up towards that. It could be hundreds of thousands of people that you influence, and that's what coaching is all about.'

EXPERIENCE

Tony expands on some examples of late where he has demonstrated this desire, with a message that all coaches and educators can take away to their work. 'I always think about meeting someone for the first time. A coach could come on a course, and this could be their first type of exposure to this theme of learning. If I don't deliver the content, or share the message in the right way, this could impact their attitude towards this format, sport or activity for the rest of their life. I know, after the amount of feedback I've had, that I hit the sweet point more times than not: the number of people I've connected with over the years who still contact me and want me to share my knowledge and give them advice today is testament to this.'

The next question for Tony is how he manages to achieve this, and the mindset that he employs to ensure that he is always delivering the best service he can. 'I want experience to be special.

'For me, it's not dissimilar from your experience in a restaurant. If I cook you a good meal, the service is friendly and you're generally enjoying the evening, then you're going to spend more time with me in the first place. Also, you might want to return at some point in the future because you want that meal again or, better yet, to try something else off the menu after the first positive experience.'

'On the contrary, if someone comes into my restaurant and eats the meal as quickly as possible, pays the bill and then is on their way out, it says to me that some aspect of the overall connection hasn't been great and I'm going to have to sit down and try and work out why that was.'

The analogy isn't a total representation of the coach-athlete relationship but, for Tony, it sums up a great deal of the nuances in the situation and gives him a great opportunity to reflect and review the performance of his courses and sessions.

INFORMATION OVERLOAD

Another difficulty with connection in the 21st century is

the pure wealth and level of information that we're bombarded with 24/7. It's crucial to know that, sometimes, we're best forming our own opinions as opposed to those that may superficially seem the obvious answer, as Tony explains. 'The important thing is that the world we live in has so much information readily available to us: I can search up a goalkeeper's name into the internet and bring up a variety of different profiles about who they supposedly are, what they've done in the past and get a well-informed idea about the type of person they are.'

'For me, though, that superficial level of understanding is not enough. Everyone is entitled to their opinions of others, and I totally respect that, but sometimes you just have to ask yourself whether you know people well enough to judge them, because that's the danger in this modern world. We spend so much time texting, emailing, even on phone calls that it has become rare to actually sit down together and have a one-to-one conversation with others. Before I make a solid judgement for or against anyone, I have to have had that sit down conversation with them, giving them an opportunity to show me perspective from their side of the table, and to start to forge that connection.'

It is clear that such shifts in communication will have implications for us as coaches, and our demeanour with our athletes, also. 'We have to make a lot more time to interact and connect, especially with our youngsters', says Tony. 'It's about understanding and adapting our current processes to the world we live in. It would be wrong of me to say "let's ignore technology", because it has such mammoth benefits when it comes to sharing information. On the other hand, it is my responsibility to deliver information across a variety of media, dependent on the athlete I'm working with and what it really is they need to develop and improve.'

In short, then, technology is an invaluable tool to add to a coaches arsenal, but should enhance and not replace our other methods of feedback, guidance and communication, to ensure that we can maintain that level of connection and bonding with our goalkeepers, which moves us smoothly along to our third chapter of the section.

Figure 17: Tony (blue) connecting with futsal goalkeeper Jordan Parker during a match.

Figure 18: Tony (light blue) delivering a futsal workshop and striving to give the best experience possible.

VII
COMMUNICATION

There's no doubt that, in modern football, the term 'communication' has become a bit of a fluffy one. It is used in every team briefing, from player-to-player and across a plethora of different culture scenes as well. The reality is, though, that the fundamental nature of communication is dependent on two elements of great substance. 'I speak a lot about communication to coaches, because it's something that is used to excuse and address possibly too many different scenarios. How many times has a kid blurted out "communication" as a coaching point, with no real idea about how or what they need to be saying?'

Regardless of whether this is on-the-pitch with your goalkeepers or off-the-field in the boardroom, communication revolves around two areas in particular: the how and the what.

HOW?

'This is the way in which you go about delivering your message', Tony explains, before listing a number of examples through which this translates: 'Is it the projection or softness of your voice? The fact you're eye-to-eye with your athletes? The environment that you create when you're working with the goalkeepers? 'There are many meaningful messages that we have to share with the goalkeepers and it's imperative that we deliver them in the best way possible.

Alternatively, it could be that you're delivering a workshop, seminar or coaching course. All of a sudden it's on your shoulders to deliver that message and information to the incoming crowds. You'll have to adapt your delivery methods to the specific group you're working with, and you'll have to make very conscious decisions about your body language, tone of voice and the terminology you use.'

WHAT?

'I'd split the what into two processes: it's the information you give, and the instruction that you use to dictate that.

This is vital to the whole process, because it's the detail and the meat on the bones. You can be as loud and as charismatic as you like, but if the detail isn't there and you're speaking rubbish, it'll be found out very quickly in the world of elite sport. Once more, it's adaptive to where you're working and the context of the conversation, because you're not going to delve into hours of detail with the goalkeeper on the pitch; it's about making sure that you can deliver the information you feel is necessary, even if you have to be very clear and concise about it.'

'Particularly as a manager or leader within a squad, the communication element and the instruction behind this becomes greatly important. The whole structure of the culture will collapse if you can't connect with people and elaborate on the messages that you want to share. I say that because it's easy to give "headlines" (small and direct 'mission statements' about where one wants the squad to go), but can you go into that greater level of detail about what you need to happen in a variety of different operational areas for the club? Is there a plan behind the dream? I think that's where many managers can fall down and it's crucial that those involved with sport are honing these skills from a young age.'

Clearly, both the 'how' and the 'what' of communication are imperative to Tony, but there is more depth to the theme than a couple of definitions.

CREDIBILITY

Tony also sees his role in communication as one that solidifies his reputation and authority with those he's working with. 'I like to judge myself by the credibility that my communication brings, because if they're trusting me and the messages that I'm sharing with them, then I've succeeded in keeping them engaged, attentive and eager to learn something around the topic I'm delivering on.'

To the contrary, there are times when Tony can sit with someone and has a little more difficulty. 'You have to ask yourself "do they really know what they're talking about?", because they're not transmitting their information with any deal of clarity or conviction,' Tony tells me, and he believes that the way in which people convey their ideas speaks volumes for the knowledge base they've built up behind the facade.

APPLICATION

Now we've broken down the 'how' and the 'what' of communication into some more detail, and hopefully started to float some reflection on how you may adapt your processes, Tony speaks to me about a couple of moments and scenarios where communication became as imperative as it was challenging. 'One of the most enlightening experiences for me was moving over to coach across the different disability formats. Deaf players in particular require an incredibly nuanced method of delivery to ensure that you're giving them the service that they deserve and that they can understand precisely what you're trying to say.'

'It can be really challenging, because often we'd be working between a sign-language translator and that adds an extra level of complexity to the communication: we had to work on a three-way process and ensure everyone was on the same page. As a coach, it made me think about how I communicated in different ways and I had to very consciously push to ensure that the messages I was conveying were accurate, precise and not leaving any room for ambiguity.'

'What can also happen in this situation, though, is that the ball-rolling time can be destroyed in an instant. All of a sudden, you've added an extra third to your communication process, which is likely to take longer regardless, given the nature of sign language. I had to make absolutely certain that I was in and out as quickly as I could, because otherwise we'd find session time slipping away very quickly.'

It is clear that working across different disability formats certainly brings a new dynamic to many elements of communication, building on the idea of empathising with the athletes and ensuring a sender-receiver connection. Perhaps it is no surprise that Tony has moved from format-to-format with relative ease?

He speaks next of another example within communication through a culture, and how through Tony had to adapt his persona, mindset and empathy levels to work with the blind squads over the past few years. 'The biggest thing that I had to understand with the blind squad was that I was entering their natural environment, and certainly not vice-versa.

'As soon as I got that job I knew that I had to restructure my behaviour and general thought process massively in order to provide the best possible service to the players. The goalkeeper was fully-sighted and a slightly different predicament, but there was a massive need to adapt for the squad as a whole. For someone who had never worked with the disabled formats at the time, it was a massive learning experience for me and one that I had to thrust myself into very quickly.'

'I immersed myself within the whole-squad group', Tony says, before moving on to talk about how he was always likely to make the odd situational faux pas. 'I had to be prepared to make mistakes, do things that might be seen as stupid, and ultimately expose myself pretty heavily to this group, because it's what would become necessary for me to understand the way that they functioned and how I could help them most.'

'Very quickly, I built up really strong relationships with many of the players, and this is the base from which the communication aspects of our connections are created.'

EMPATHY

'The crucial element to get right is being able to empathise with the athletes and people that you're working with. When I took the job with the blind squad, my only previous interaction with anything similar to the format was a one-day blind futsal course, and so it really was an area that I had very little information about. Everything that I would do, therefore, would be litmus-tested against world-class athletes - some of whom had competed in two Paralympics. If I hadn't been able to understand the situation from their perspective and identify the manner through which I needed to communicate very quickly, it could've been a real disaster.'

In order to create this learning platform for Tony and his players, I ask about the support Tony had from the team itself. 'The boys were brilliant. They could have dug me out massively, especially given their experience and reputation. I think that they understood, though, the help that I could bring them and therefore were willing to be patient and allow me to explore the different realms of communication and tactics that could work best with the group.'

'There was also a good deal of banter around times where I might make a mistake. It was never a case of "this is shocking, you're not allowed to do that", but instead they realised that it probably wasn't intentional and so just made light of the situation by sending a little jibe my way.'

'One particular example that I remember is that we really take for granted the capabilities that we have and what we can do. Sometimes, I remember that I'd walk through a door, and leave it behind me, just assuming that whoever was coming through next could deal with it themselves. Of course, for a blind player, they're probably going to be recreating their journey based on their past experiences. So, if the door was open last time they tried to come through it, I'm going to have created a little bit of a problem for them! That's where you have to really think in the shoes of the other person, and I think that my experience with the blind squad in this regard developed many of the empathetic areas of my communication.'

After hearing Tony talk around the subject in more detail, it fascinates me that there are so many different domains over which application of communication must be honed. In each separate scenario, different skills will be focused on. Coaches can then combine and draw upon these to become the best possible communicators in their field. The most important aspect, though, is the deliberation with which you represent yourself and deliver your message, as Tony explains next.

WAITING FOR THE RIGHT TIME

'In summary, communication comes down to your manner

and the trust that you instil within your players: how much are they willing to commit to your processes and the messages that you have to share?'

'Some of the buy-in will come from reputation or shared experience, but the most important element will be the medium through which you deliver your message', believes Tony, although this will have to be adjusted for the picture in front of you. 'When there are such a wide variety of roles, responsibilities and positions within a club, it can be difficult, but it's all about identifying which context suits which group best and then taking steps to transfer your message from there.'

Tony also understands that there is a correct time for that information to come, whether that be tactical instruction or a logistical operation. 'I don't think it's ever a case of forcing information out of me, because that's counterproductive and may well be inefficient for the player. Instead, I'm more likely to say "what information do you need to help better yourself?", and then I can start to tap into the metaphorical hard-drive from there.'

'It's imperative that coaches are very deliberate about the context of their conversations', explains Tony, 'and we have to create the best possible environments to support that. For example, it might be a case of a one-to-one chat like we're having here over a coffee, or maybe it will be a small group of individuals where you can brainstorm and align your vision moving forward.'

I ask Tony, finally, for the most pivotal aspect of communication that coaches should strive to improve first and foremost. 'The key is always how you come across to the receiver: how you impress yourself towards them. And then it's just about deciding what to share at what moment - do they need it for the game? Will it support their development?' That's communication, through the eyes of Tony.

Figure 19: Tony (middle) communicating with his goalkeepers on the court, ensuring that they understand the messages that need to be delivered.

Figure 20: Tony (front) changing his communication style to work with a whole group environment: he is also making the aids at his disposal work for him to simplify the communication process.

VIII
CONFIDENCE

Similar to the communication elements that we looked at in the previous chapter, Tony believes that the word confidence is too heavily used in the footballing world. It has large psychological significance, and maybe a much more complex domain than that with which it is usually associated. A plethora of different factors influence the level of confidence that performers have. This might be state-specific (i.e in the context of the game), but it could be something well away from football or even an innate disposition, depending on which side of the psychological fence that you sit.

'Sometimes we forget that sportsmen and women are people as well, and there's so much going on in their lives that could erupt at any one particular moment', Tony explains during our conversation. You can see that there is a glint of something deep in his eyes.

'Sport becomes the solace and freedom for so many people. I've been there and appreciate how hard it is; athletes should treat sport as their opportunity to have a greater level of freedom and shut away all the issues they may be facing. Part of the job of the coach is to build up that sense of confidence in the players, and make the environment one in which it is conducive to letting go of your fears and issues.

Tony is clear that this can be of huge benefit to the players. 'It's a massive support for players, goalkeepers especially, because there's often so much happening in their lives, that having this platform to just enjoy, thrive and love the game of football again is unprecedented.'

'You have to be careful, though', heeds Tony, 'because it might be that the problems of one individual in terms of confidence could have an unquantifiable impact on the whole squad, and this is where your role as a coach might extend itself a little further.

'It's going to revolve around knowing your individual and having built up that mutual connection - you might have to utilise that to probe the positivity and try to support the thinking mechanisms of the player. There could be some real personal issues within the squad, that only a small cluster of people are party to. For the support staff, it's about the recognition of where and when is an appropriate opportunity to tackle these situations, and what the best possible route of action is: should information be shared with the whole group or are we best just to isolate it? Shared experiences and relationships offered by the whole group can really help the individual in difficulty come to terms with whatever their issues might be, and achieving that balance of sensitivity and holistic support is imperative.'

NERVES

'We all prepare ourselves for football in different ways', Tony tells me, as we start to delve into his processes to deal with the pre-match anxiety he would feel. 'I struggled with nerves and confidence massively as a player. There aren't too many people in the world who know this, but I used to vomit before every game of football that I ever played in. That was a mechanism for me to release my nervousness, and then walk down the tunnel and be able to play.'

'I'm not sure if it was habit or just an anchor to rely on, but sometimes it would draw out onto the pitch as well... There were instances where in the first few minutes of the game I was physically retching, because I hadn't properly got over the sickness in the changing rooms and felt the need to release it pitch-side instead. Luckily, there was only one occasion - where I was genuinely ill as opposed to nervous - where I was actually sick on the pitch.'

'Is that confidence? Is it nervousness? Is it anxiety?' Tony ponders for a moment. 'That's the difficulty of confidence as a word. There are so many descriptives that fit within it and so many different ways of dealing with the problems that it can create.'

BREAKING BARRIERS

'Ultimately, as a coach, if you have built up a strong enough relationship and connection with a given individual, and they have a really deep level of trust in your personal standards, then the majority of the time you'll be able to break down the barriers and face the obstacles or issues that they might be facing, whether that's a quick-fix or a long-lasting problem.'

There are a variety of ways to help reduce this barrier for a player-coach relationship, and Tony is very open about some of the techniques he has used with goalkeepers over the years. 'One thing for me is as simple as changing the environment: players are likely to be much more relaxed and at ease on the training ground than they might be in the classroom, so why not use this as your opportunity to bounce a few thoughts around them and help them talk about the issues they might be facing?'

'Alternatively, you could use the support mechanisms (sports psychologists) within the squad, to help prepare and understand the players on a deeper level. There are some things that we obviously can't talk about, but if it's an issue that's influencing performance in the way it manifests itself on the pitch, then I believe a shared, trusted approach is ideal for supporting the goalkeeper through this difficult stage.'

'At the end of the day, it might not be an issue for me to deal with - maybe it's something I identify and then pass on to the psychologist who can try to tackle that with the individual goalkeeper.'

TRUST

To facilitate the joint process of recovering and building confidence, Tony's sure that trust must be an underpinning foundation in the way in which relationships are developed.

'As much as we trust the goalkeepers we're working with in the sense of delegation and giving them ownership on the pitch, the goalkeepers also trust us massively to be delivering the right knowledge to them, standing up for them in the dressing room and also having the confidence to support the goalkeeper when the finger is not being fairly pointed at them.' That voice, or face at least, in the dressing room can go an awful long way when it seems as though all the chips are down for the goalkeeper, and Tony has certainly held that role enough times to know how it feels. All of a sudden, an isolated and secular position has a supporting body to guide, advise and ensure it's headed in the right direction. Within some structures, though, the authoritative nature within backroom teams can create difficulty for the goalkeeper coach, who's often caught between a rock and a hard place.

'It's really important, for me, to back your own beliefs', Tony replies when I ask him how he may deal with this situation. 'If that means that the head coach is incorrectly questioning or finding fault with the goalkeeper, and you have to express that, then that might well be the case. You've got to stick to task, back who you believe was right in a given situation, and make sure that you're being as loyal as you can to the goalkeeper: you're his or her biggest and most learned voice within that squad. I've had a couple of awkward situations where I might have been pushed into a corner as a goalkeeper coach and asked to deal with matters in a certain way, which might lead to losing the goalkeeper.'

'You can question yourself in these times because it's very difficult having to play the politics game, but it just helps you put into perspective that understanding of what it really does mean to back your goalkeepers and why it's so important for them to feel and understand your support as well.'

Tony sees trust as part of the communication process: it's all about building a rapport through which a message can be sent. Running parallel to these skills, surely, is the ability to show and command commitment from those with whom you work.

IX

COMMITMENT

Commitment is something to be commanded and to display. It comes from the deepest depth of a team's motivation and will be a vital cog in determining their success. Steiner's 1972 model of group dynamics gives particular weight to the importance of reducing 'faulty processes': lack of commitment to the cause is one that we see reeking havoc every day. Beyond the science of psychology and management, though, commitment has a firm grounding within what is often seen as the 'art of leadership': how can you drive your team to work for, with and towards the same goals as you?

WOLVES

Tony talks about this both from the perspective as a leader and as a coach. His aim, as always, is to help others on their journey to success and betterment of the group. 'Somebody recently put an image on social media about a pack of wolves. There were twenty or so of them walking through the tundra, with the weakest at the front, followed by a strong group in the middle, and the absolute warrior - the leader of the pack - bringing up the rear from the back. It surprised me at first, because it was a little abstract and not how we would consider traditional leadership.'

'It gave me a great opportunity to reflect about the way that we conduct ourselves as coaches and what commitment to the cause might actually look like: it's not necessarily pushing yourself ahead of everyone else. The wolves were doing an incredible job here. They were ensuring that nobody would be left behind, but the leader of the pack was also able to drive forward and enthuse the group to keep working, instilling a great deal of commitment both through his personal behaviours and also in the sense that he's seen to put others ahead of himself.'

'Within a squad, it's about recognising where this vulnerability might lie, and then facilitating and accommodating your team to recognise and work within this.

The most important thing for me, though, is that no two packs will ever be the same'. The same applies to squads of football, believes Tony.

ALIGNED GOALS

'As a coach, I've worked with so many different people and leaders, all of whom have had their own ideologies as to how they work with the group and achieve that level of commitment. 'Sometimes a group of players have different views and expectations to the leader, or different understandings of the nuances of a given position. In these scenarios, the leader has a massive job in helping to realign the commitment of the team towards one common goal, and there are a multitude of different tools in his or her arsenal to achieve that.'

'It might involve a shift in the environment: what vibes are we giving off about our culture as a setup? On other occasions, it might be something as simple as a team meeting to discuss goals, objectives and targets for the coming season or cycle, making sure the players know absolutely what's expected of them and how the squad aims to work together to achieve that.'

Tony is also quick to recognise that not every team has a squad of 20 players, chomping at the bit to demonstrate their commitment to wearing the club badge. In these scenarios, and when Tony and I speak about how to build a culture of commitment, he stresses that a lot of the time the seeds are planted very early on within the process. 'I think sometimes it needs a good level of personal selection, and then to create a really strong buy-in beyond that.'

He mentions a number of environments where this buy-in has been evident, from shared targets and goals that are embedded into the team philosophy, to the sense of international pride with some of the squads he's coached with. 'I feel an absolute honour when I'm singing the national anthem for my country, and this feeling and emotion should be mirrored with the players as well: a lot of their commitment should be towards the three lions: it's a brilliant way to channel their dedication.' Maybe, we discuss, clubs and coaches can start to think about what it means to represent a particular organisation. Whether it be an academy, grassroots or elite senior team, coaches having the opportunity to pull on the unique aspects of their club culture can really pay dividends for promoting social cohesion and aligning players towards common goals.

UNIFIED INDIVIDUALITY

Tony has already spoken at great length about his personal

motivations, his family, and why he continues to push himself in the coaching world, but there has to be an understanding of commitment from the coach to the team, too. 'Looking at a coach's personal perspective, it's all about wanting to be involved with a setup for the right reasons. Having that desire to win, to be the best that you can be.'

He is quick to add, also, that it's not just about personal success and triumphs. 'Whenever we go off to a major tournament, it doesn't worry me if I don't have a medal around my neck at the end of it whilst the players are delighted with the trophy. My drive is seeing the players become the absolute best that they can be, after hours and hours of practice on the training ground and then during the tournaments as well. It's not my place to celebrate their successes for them.'

'My commitment, therefore, hopefully manifests itself in my behaviour to support and aid these players: it's about getting them up on that medal podium, ultimately showing just quite what they've achieved through concentrated effort and dedication.

Building on that, Tony makes it clear that he doesn't believe that he has to go out of his way to demonstrate that commitment in public: it's about letting the work do the talking. 'It's not my belief that a coach should have to scream and shout about their commitment and how driven they are towards the team's goals.

'It should be implicitly obvious and recognised from their behaviours and the way they go about representing themselves with professionalism and determination, grounded in a great deal of humility.'

INSPIRATION

I ask Tony, then, if he believes a coach should be inspirational to create commitment, and how far he would take that statement. 'There's a difference between being inspirational and having an ego', Tony points out. 'Having an ego suggests that you're the kind of individual who lives off their past, talking about it at every moment and implying that they have some kind of divine advantage just because of what they've done before.'

'Inspiration is about being the best that you can be. I love my family and I get a tingle in my stomach whenever I talk about them; it makes me well up. They are my inspiration and the reason that I do what I do and have driven myself to carve out the career that I've had.'

The metric for Tony's success, then, takes a slightly different perspective. 'To improve myself, I've got to improve others. That's what my success is determined by. Inspiration is about being nice, a good person, looking after my wife and kids and knowing that I'd die for them if I needed to, because that's what my life is about.' As Tony says this, I can't help but feel that there is no exaggeration in what he is declaring. 'Inspiring the people that I come into contact with is so important for me, and helping to reduce or negate some of the negativity and evil that there is in the world, with humility and gratefulness at the forefront.'

Being a former professional himself, I ask if Tony uses that to inspire and build the commitment of his athletes. 'I try not to talk about playing too much with my goalkeepers, because that might not particularly be the inspiration that they want or need. Instead, I just appreciate the experiences, learnings and findings that it has given me, which shape and mould the character I am today.'

'What I try to do is to use those experiences to the betterment of others through storytelling and imagery, often helping that goalkeeper commit to you because you can relate over your past. It's a lot about gauging what's going to make the goalkeepers you're surrounded by tick. They might be fascinated and technically interested in some of the experiences that I've undertaken, in which case I've got no problem sharing who I played against and how we dealt with it. On the other hand, it's not my job to thrust the name-dropping of international stars into a conversation, just because I want the goalkeeper to believe in how good I used to be.'

As we draw towards a summary of commitment, I ask Tony

one more question.

'When we're working at the top-level in elite sport, how much of a gain does commitment offer? Would you value it as marginal, or fundamental?'

'At the end of the day, if the players or coaches aren't committed, then you're never going to express yourself in your best form - life becomes a trivial and pointless exercise', replies Tony, taking a tangent that I certainly hadn't expected. 'It's not necessarily about the gains it brings us on the pitch (which no doubt will be substantial), but more the recognition that we've only got a very finite number of years on this planet, and these are best spent doing something that we're committed towards and have a real passion to proving ourselves within.'

X

YOUR ATHLETES

On a closing note, Tony and I both agree that it is impossible simply to discuss a variety of different pillars within building relationships without giving some more guidance about how these can be formulated and adjusted for each athlete. Tony puts getting the most out of his athletes into two brackets: intuition, and a bespoke approach.

INTUITION

One great quality that Tony sees in coaches is the ability to think intuitively, through deciphering information and using past experiences to guide one's actions. Their is scientific validation behind the phenomenon of 'going with your gut', and Tony grounds this through his anecdotal emotions and personal experiences. It is imperative to communicating with, respecting and connecting with your athletes and will help you to build close bonds and bridges with those that you work with.

EMOTIONAL INTELLIGENCE

'For me, going with the gut is all about your emotional intelligence as a person. Over my 47 years on this planet, I've had experiences and challenges: many positive and many negative. These experiences are all stored over time and will become the foundation from which I behave and make decisions in the future.' Tony is clear that past experiences are useful beyond their initial moment, as a tool both for reflection and for memory. 'You learn from them massively. In similar future scenarios, you gain a really good idea of how to deal with the situation and there is almost an instinctive feeling of what's right and what's wrong, whether that's on the football pitch or away from it.'

'Sometimes, logic is very helpful and often using your head is a necessary part of the process. However, life doesn't come with a manual, and there's certainly no set path for one individual to take. It might not always be a case of doing things as we're told they should be. We can't be afraid to trust the gut: navigating situations, careers or personal experiences in a new direction can bear many fruits later down the line.'

'Again, it comes down to this aspect of trusting and understanding the situations in which you have accrued experience from. It's crucial, also, to have the understanding that the gut decisions you make won't always be right', says Tony, before he goes on to talk about the ways in which 'incorrect' decisions can be the catalyst for future change.

'A vital part of the process of being able to use and trust the gut is actually making mistakes. There has to be a failure and feedback mechanism within the system in order to allow you to make the right choice in the future, when you're more experienced and have more options to think about.'

Tony appreciates that individuals who naturally struggle with making intuitive decisions might shy away from them in the future, after a number of rash, impulsive or unfavourable calls. He believes, though, that success will come when coaches have the confidence to continue working with intuition. 'Believing in your gut instinct is the predisposition for its use, in my opinion. The second fundamental is to have the experiences of a lifetime, which will help you to make correct and informed decisions, due to the fact that you can remember and call upon past experience to find the solution to whatever your problem may be.'

CURVEBALLS

Often, we might view this idea of automatic processing, using memorised solutions to solve problems, and calling upon past experience to mould future behaviours as a topic best suited for the skill acquisition pages of this book. However, as Tony very rightly points out, intuition has an equally 'bigger picture' context to it: we can apply some of the same skill acquisition theories from the goalmouth to a coach's practice and life in general.

'It means that when life throws you a curveball, you've got the mechanisms to dodge it, and react faster because you've noticed it earlier in the environment.' A fitting analogy, even if not comprehensive.

Years on the planet, though, does not guarantee a strong intuition: it's about what you do with those years that counts. 'Some people will be so ignorant to the environment around them that they'll be totally closed to the methods, ideas or advice from other people, and this creates a situation where the gut instinct becomes rather inept.'

'If you're living such a blinkered life, and haven't used the experiences from the sharing of other individuals to build your past experience and knowledge to the point that it's at today, how can you expect to have the range of variables within your mind to be able to trust your gut and the decisions it makes?'

Different perspectives, and the opportunity to reflect on those you hold personally, add extra tools to the arsenal and supports the ability of a person to make the right gut decision at the right moment. Experience alone, therefore, is not enough.

BESPOKE APPROACH

Secondly, the overarching idea that underlines all of the group and individual dynamics that we've looked at is the ability to adapt and mould your interpersonal skills dependent on the athlete that's stood in front of you. Without this ability to change the way you deliver your message or try to gather their commitment, your work will become defunct and inefficient. As Tony says: 'it's all about what makes a particular person tick'.

UNDERNEATH THE SURFACE

'We're all individuals, and no two people are absolutely identical in their personality nor appearance', declares Tony. 'Some of us are introvert, some of us struggle with situations of great pressure, and some of us will have a great ability to connect with and build rapport with those around us. As a leader, then, beyond even the technical differences on the football pitch, it's about connection and truly understanding the individual so that you can have the best possible impact on them, across all the areas that we've already mentioned. What does that person want, or need, to experience in a given moment?' It would be impossible to generate a formula for this experience, as it will vary so fluidly from player to player, and Tony remembers that the person behind the football boots is also of crucial importance.

'When we're spending so much time working in a team environment and concerned with culture and tactics, sometimes we can forget about what really matters: the person on the other side of that white line. How much do we really know about the people who we're asking to push their bodies to the marginal limits of performance?', asks Tony. 'If you can get little bits of knowledge and detail around the identity of your athletes, maybe their parents, partners or family, then you will be able to create and build an environment where you can ensure a player-centred approach to their needs, but also a culture where it's really palpably obvious that you care about the people you're working with.'

'If you just rock up and deliver a session, regardless of the technical outcomes from it, the goalkeeper is going to come away with a very different impression to if you'd spent some time before or afterwards building up that relationship across a holistic variety of details and information points.'

In further conversation, it became apparent that there are an abundance of ways in which it is clear that Tony adapts his practice and demeanour based on who he's working with. By no means is it an easy skill to achieve, but one of the first-stepping stones to relating to those you're working with can be to put yourself not just in their shoes, but in their life as well:

> How many hours have they travelled to reach this session?
>
> Have they come to this session after a long day of exams at school?
>
> Have they just had an argument with their partner?
>
> Have they just returned from long-term injury?
>
> What hobbies do they have beyond goalkeeping?
>
> Why are they playing sport in the first place?
>
> What personality traits can we establish?

Only once we can start to understand these questions, and build up a holistic view of this player's perspective can we offer that truly tailored and bespoke approach to our coaching and communications with them. Depending on your situation with the athlete will impact how you try and deduce this information, but it could be something as simple as a conversation on the walk to the car park to the training ground or a quick bite of lunch before or after a training session.

Through these opportunities, the connection, commitment and respect from your athletes will multiply, helping you to imprint your philosophy and ethos upon their play and performance, becoming much more apparent in the next section.

Section Three

Building a syllabus

XI
CREATING A GOALKEEPING PHILOSOPHY

Over Tony's many years in the game, it would seem as though he has developed a rather unique and instrumental ability to compile and create goalkeeping syllabuses, philosophies and models with great impact on those that he is working with. Whether it be creating a programme for the futsal goalkeepers with no prior experience in the sport or putting models of talent development in place from Tony's latest role within the women's game, there is certainly no shortage of expertise and knowledge to tap into in this section. We will speak about Tony's personal philosophies, the importance of these methodologies within an organisation's structure, and also a little bit more in the way of framework for building these up so you can create a representative and fulfilling philosophy of your own game. We start, of course, with the philosophy itself.

ELEMENT ONE

'Improving goalkeeper development by giving goalkeepers the technical skill set and knowledge they require.'

'These are your tools of the trade', remarks Tony. 'If you're an outfield player, one of the first things you'll learn how to do is to control the football, because you can't run, dribble and shoot top-corner until you've got the fundamentals in place! All we're doing, in reality, is giving goalkeepers the tools they require to work from in order to have the best possible chance of saving the ball - it's like the golfing analogy we spoke of earlier.' It's clear from having the opportunity to observe some of Tony's practices that purposeful technique plays a great part in the way in which he operates, building goalkeepers to deal with the pressures of elite-level sport.

His depth and detail across a multitude of different facets is unrivalled to anything I've seen before, and the way his goalkeepers speak of this diligence to preparation and success is quite eye-opening. 'The more areas of detail that I can give to my goalkeeper - at the appropriate moment - the better, in my opinion. As the goalkeeper coach, part of my role is to understand the technical requirements of the goalkeepers I'm working with and ensure that we can develop and enhance them in that regard.' However, it is imperative that the technical training we're doing is relevant to the goalkeeper's needs on the pitch, adds Tony: 'What's the point in practicing technique for the sake of practicing technique? There isn't one. We need to ensure that the technical practices our goalkeepers are working with have a direct relation to what they're likely to see on a match-day.'

ELEMENT TWO

'Taking a holistic approach to physical talent identification within goalkeeping.'

Tony has spent time working across a wealth of different formats, all with varying physical capabilities and requirements. When he talks of the 'all-round' physical goalkeeper, his argument certainly holds a great deal of weight: 'Around eight or nine years ago, academies suddenly decided that they needed giants in the goal; the kind of kids who are

6" tall as a 12- or 13-year-old. Ultimately, though, you have to ask a very fundamental question here: is the tallest goalkeeper necessarily the best?' Tony reminisces of his childhood, where many of his idols were venturing under 6". 'I go back to when I was a kid, avidly watching football and scrutinising the goalkeepers... They weren't 6"4, without a doubt, more like 5"10 or 5"11, with the likes of Paul Cooper and Peter Fox hanging around the 5"9 mark.'

'Having said that, what these goalkeepers did have was an incredible level of athleticism, jumping height and flexibility. Using their attributes, they were able to have a large amount of success in the goal, but probably had an adapted technical base to what we see with goalkeepers now.'

Tony is careful, though, to understand that the game has changed and the modern-day goalkeeper can use height to their advantage. 'Yes, if goalkeepers are head and shoulders above the others there will be many benefits to that, but I don't believe that factors like athleticism, technical skill set and the raw materials of a goalkeeper should be neglected in search of a towering presence: they may well be frightened to death of coming for crosses, or be more cumbersome than a smaller keeper because of the length of their limbs and coordination.' The message to take here, then, is without a doubt that physicality is important for the goalkeeper, but must be managed, targeted and identified in the context of all-round ability and holistic physical components, as opposed to merely filtering goalkeeping ability - or potential - based on the height that goalkeepers may be predicted to stand at; it's what they do with the height they have that counts.

ELEMENT THREE

'Introducing the development of new movements, skills and passes, specific to the role of the goalkeeper in the ever-evolving game.'

The idea of introducing natural movement patterns for any athletes is imperative from an early age, but Tony goes on here to talk about its importance at the elite-level of the game, as well as how - and why - some goalkeeper coaches aren't getting it right at the moment. 'I've seen a number of pieces of work recently where the session design and practice is probably more akin to a circus. There are hurdles, poles, cones and duct tape absolutely everywhere - you could say it has the feeling of an airport landing strip!' Tony's absolutely not denouncing the importance of movement for the goalkeeper, but he does have ideas around the fundamentals from which it should stem: 'In my opinion, the goalkeepers simply have to be moving in a natural way. Any new ideas or thoughts I have around practices are for mobility, for speed or for the specific movements that we know the goalkeeper has to make; they're not just in place to look good or make my video attractive for a YouTube channel.'

The goalkeeper's role as the '11th player' certainly adjusts their required capabilities in all areas of the game of football, but also requires a number of different movement patterns. 'Goalkeepers have to cover a lot of ground around the goal area, and this is growing with the idea that goalkeepers are an extra asset to their team in possession. I'm not sure that goalkeeper coaches give enough consideration to this element of movement practice and tactical understanding, meaning that we have goalkeepers expected to play in a new role without having been given the guidance and support to execute it effectively.' It's the same in sports like futsal (where the goalkeeper is expected to defend the D and defensive half in possession), too, and Tony believes it's imperative that a goalkeeper coach can allow their athletes to explore these areas in more detail and practice the movements and technical skills they require.

ELEMENT FOUR

'Ensuring that the goalkeeper is physically and tactically prepared to deal with the evolutions in the game.'

For Tony, this additional push towards outfield work for the goalkeeper also lends itself to a differing combination of requirements for the position, particularly from a physiological perspective. 'Anaerobic work will still make up the majority of an elite goalkeeper's training, but I think there's a bit of a shift at the moment to slightly more aerobic functionality, in order to ensure that goalkeepers have got the reserves and depths to deal with connecting the back four and acting as a sweeper at the same time.'

However, Tony is quick to point out that the goalkeeper's number one priority remains constant. 'First and foremost, your goalkeeper has to have speed, agility and power in order to protect the goal; everything on top of that is a bonus.'

On a slight tangent, I also question whether a 'goalkeeping department' model is likely to start evolving within the elite reaches of the game, as technology and sports science progresses so rapidly. 'Yeah, I think they already are. There are a couple of different structures where there are supporting goalkeeping coaches that specialise in different areas says Tony. 'A great example of this is at AFC Bournemouth. A good friend of mine Neil Moss is currently the lead goalkeeping coach, but they've also integrated Anthony White into the system, who has gone to great lengths to immerse and develop himself personally around the physiological elements of the game, meaning he now holds a role that specialises in sports science for the goalkeepers.'

'Of course, this is a much more feasible plan in the Premier League, where the budgets are a world away from lower down the leagues, but I think it shows the direction that goalkeeping is going, and the need for clubs to have expertise across a variety of different development and performance areas.'

From a tactical viewpoint, the goalkeeper's role can often be simplified to 'playing out from the back' or 'defending the space behind defenders'.

The reality, though, is that the tactical requirements of the goalkeeper are dynamic, complex and rapidly developing. 'The game's changing: there are so many different styles of play now that lend themselves to different positioning, distribution choices and goalkeeping philosophies. We're reaching the point where people are starting to see the goalkeeper not just as a shot-stopper, but as a multi-faceted and multi-functional individual, who can play with both their feet and their hands, as well as understanding and adapting to the setup of the opposition to have the most success.'

I push Tony for an example in this regard; he doesn't hesitate with his response. 'Pepe Reina. What a wonderful goalkeeper with his feet. He could exploit weaknesses in the opposition with his range and accuracy of passing, but also in his ability to manage the game, based on the scenario. His experience towards the latter end of his career has assisted him with this, but I think tactically he is a very, very advanced goalkeeper across a variety of different areas.'

It is clear that the role of the goalkeeper coach, in Tony's opinion, is to facilitate a great deal of this tactical proficiency, whether that be through briefing the goalkeepers or assisting them in their search for ownership themselves, and that the goalkeeper - therefore - must also be used to a larger extent in team practices, allowing them to embed and become immersed in the squad philosophies, team tactics and, ultimately, club culture.

ELEMENT FIVE

'Recognising the importance of decision-making and psychological preparation for the goalkeeper.'

Subtly eluded to in a couple of the preceding philosophy areas, the role of the goalkeeper coach in recognising, reflecting on and enhancing decision-making within a game is crucial to a goalkeeper's success, without a doubt. Tony sees the goalkeeper, in this regard, as a chess player: carefully deliberating and predicting future play, whilst trying to nullify the opposition before they have the opportunity to strike in possession.

'Always with a full view of the pitch in front of them, the

goalkeeper can see the pieces on the board, always trying to predict the next move. We've advanced beyond a goalkeeper only worrying about the final third now, so anytime there's a turnover in possession the goalkeeper is questioning themselves as to what their role is, how they can positively support play and the mindset of their positioning.'

'Once more, it comes down to the fact that there are so many elements to the modern game that are appreciated and recognised: it amplifies the decision-making process massively.'

'The message to really hammer home, I suppose, is that it's not just about keeping the ball out of the net, but also supporting the team in as many other channels as possible.'

ELEMENT SIX

'To create multi-functional, physically-developed and game-changing goalkeepers.'

Culminating the previous five points, Tony summarises his philosophy into the three above compound adjectives. It's fascinating to understand how this may well have changed over the past 10, 15 or 20 years, where previously coaches would've likely prioritised 'technical models' and 'height in isolation' as their criteria for success. Whilst Tony understands that achieving this holistically developed goalkeeper isn't always possible - nor solely influenced by the goalkeeper coach - he speaks very prudently about the role that coaches can have in prioritising development and ensuring the best performance levels.

'As the old adage goes, you can only work with what you've got. Therefore, your ability to fulfil the ideas behind the philosophy will go hand-in-hand with the goalkeepers you're working with. It might be a case where you're working with a specific goalkeeper who's constraints and anatomy mean that they won't succeed across the board, so it's the coach's role to assess and decipher what areas of development to focus on. They have to work out what will bring the biggest margin of gains for the goalkeeper.'

'Some goalkeepers are just great shot-stoppers but have never made a conscious attempt to improve the way they distribute the ball and support their team in possession - this could give you a starting point very easily. On the other hand, you might have a young lad who's played outfield for a number of years before transitioning to be a goalkeeper. You're going to have a real challenge on your hands here to give them the skill-set to deal with the ball from waist upwards effectively!'

'The goalkeeper coach might have a dozen different goalkeepers through the club he's delivering in, all with different requirements, strengths and prioritised weaknesses: how are you going to fit and support those individuals?', asks

Tony.

'It's certainly a challenge', confirms Tony, answering his own question. 'But that's the way the goalkeeper coach's role is moving: they're expected to be able to deliver over a multitude of different technical, physical, tactical and psychological elements, with an integration of social development as well. If the goalkeeper coach is not multi-functional, and prepared to go out of their way to immerse themselves in the game, learn from past experience and really absorb knowledge from the position, they're going to struggle massively with the requirements of coaching in the modern day.'

THE SUPPORTING PHILOSOPHY

It's understandable that the suggestion of a second philosophy, solely for one specific player on the pitch, may seem a little unnecessary. The supporting philosophy, though, ties together and allows the overall goalkeeping philosophies to be actioned: one is a framework for developing goalkeepers; the other related to their specific actions on the pitch in various situations.

'When you look at the supporting philosophy', adds Tony, 'you have to appreciate that it's an in-depth breakdown of the game itself. You're starting to venture into the constructs of the systems involved. The goalkeeper is part of a large number of those patterns - we've already established that their role is not merely to keep the ball out of the goal.'

In order to help paint a picture or spark an idea of how you may choose to develop your supporting philosophy, Tony and I spoke about an example of the progression of play in possession.

AN EXEMPLAR GOALKEEPING PHILOSOPHY - IN POSSESSION

The goalkeeper should act as an outfield player and be brave enough to trust team members to start the attack but always available to connect.

Simple and effective decision-making should be complimented with consistent technical execution and a range of distribution in order to retain possession.

The goalkeeper's decision process will be dependent on opposition defending strategies but must influence them by stretching teams through a switch of play or positive penetrative play to eliminate units.

During all aspects of the in-possession philosophy, defensive security should be considered.

Awareness of defensive security ensures the team remains organised at all times and can react effectively when the ball is lost.

All players contribute to ensuring defensive security, in particular the goalkeeper through effective positioning, organisation and communication.

Without wanting to overload goalkeepers with technical and tactical information that they will not be able to retain, it is imperative that the goalkeeper has a role within the phases of play and understands this. 'It might not always be with the ball', says Tony, 'but the goalkeeper will always be influencing the shape of the opposition, the opportunity for transition, and a whole host of other variables.' This is where the supporting philosophy impacts on the team's performance, and Tony is convinced that it differs between individual goalkeepers and formats of the game.

'In mainstream football, the areas are bigger and wider, which probably acts to increase the time of decision-making for the goalkeeper. Futsal, on the other hand, is a totally different sport, because the play can switch from 'D' to 'D' in three to five seconds. It's a rapid turnover that requires even faster decision-making; there simply isn't any time for hesitation. Therefore, the two sports have very different requirements from the goalkeeper's supporting philosophy and we give the goalkeeper a great deal of focus and objectivity by stating it explicitly.'

XII
ETHOS

The idea of an ethos may not be one that many have discussed or considered in too much detail. More of an overarching guide to moral standards than anything else: a job specification that holds true, regardless of where a coach is working. Unsurprisingly, Tony sees his ethos as his tool for ensuring integrity, diligence and optimum performance everywhere he works.

'Responsibility is a massive part of why I create the ethos. If I'm talking to a coach and sharing my goalkeeping philosophy, for example, I'm responsible for the information that they're receiving and have to ensure that it is as validated and accurate as possible. It's like the accountability that I feel when delivering a Level One goalkeeper course - this contact could be the first real exposure the learner has to coach education, and that experience has to a memorable one for them.'

Further, it is apparent that Tony feels a great deal of magnitude around his behaviours (which lead into his ethos), as a coach, and that these can have far-reaching consequences. 'If I relay the wrong information to them, have the wrong attitude towards the course or take away some vital learning experiences, I could potentially disrupt their coaching journey for the rest of their life. Whether they're inspired to go on and coach in the Premier League or whether they stop coaching on a Tuesday evening is partly on my shoulders: it's all about their fulfilment, enjoyment, understanding, and detail.'

ELEMENT ONE

'The goalkeeper coach must have a vision and understand the goalkeeper's role.'

As we sit, in a room lined with goalkeeping biographies, coaching manuals and DVDs in the bookcases (alongside the biggest personal film collection I've ever seen!), Tony seems to click slightly when he talks of the importance of the goalkeeper coach learning and discovering what he desires from the game. 'I think it links in massively to the resources out there and how much people are willing to learn. It's not necessarily about hoarding every book, blog article or course under the sun and declaring that you're now a goalkeeping expert, but it's about taking the key messages from these manuals, from conversations with mentors and from ideas from your travels. The most important thing is that you then action and execute based on your findings.'

'Over the years, I've exposed myself to as many different formats, opinions and perspectives as possible. Some of them are incredible, and others you wouldn't want to use if your life depended on it.' I ask Tony, then, whether he thinks he should streamline further the information he takes in, as well as that which he executes, in order to build up depth and detail across certain areas. 'I don't think so, no. I've found so much value over the years from speaking to a plethora of different people, all with a multitude of opinions on the world of goalkeeping across different formats of the game; I wouldn't be the coach I am now without that wide berth of knowledge and perspective.'

For Tony, it's very clear that he believes there's no 'one way' of coaching goalkeepers. Following the idea that every individual has reached their coaching philosophies from a different path, he speaks about the evolution in learning pathways over the last few decades, and how that's helped to develop his vision and understanding as a coach. 'My era of learning and playing as a goalkeeper is totally different to the environment that goalkeepers are in now. I learned an awful lot during that time from incredible mentors, coaches and colleagues. However it's also imperative that I keep myself up-to-date with the progressions of the game and the transformations it's undergone.'

I ask about these transformations. 'Coaching has changed in the way it's delivered as a science, the content of coach education that we're expected to give to our players and the evolution of the game, which naturally causes a different coaching style and methodology to emerge over time.'

'As a coach working across many different formats, I've been dragged along with a lot of this evolution, I believe. There was an awful lot of work that I ploughed through when starting off in the futsal format, because it's such a different game, and since that I've used these skills to transfer my research methods across all five the formats in which I've worked. I'm very glad that I didn't choose to specialise in mainstream football in the beginning, because I think it would have been much easier to hide away from the learning and knowledge-building that has supported me so prominently on my journey.'

There also, though, has to be an understanding that not all of a coach's learnings and experiences are relevant in any one scenario. 'It's about being able to take and adapt what you know to the situation you're faced with', explains Tony. 'Part of the skill of building up the knowledge base is the idea of when to separate it, when to mix it with other ideas you've got and when it's not necessary at all. There's a fine line, and that's why it's so much about your understanding of why you make the decisions you do.'

ELEMENT TWO

'Dealing with and supporting the role of the goalkeeper and surrounding units in the team's playing system.'

More than ever before, the goalkeeper coach is expected to understand, support and deliver on a wide-ranging list of components within the game, a significant part of which revolves around the goalkeeper's integration in the team's playing style and philosophy. It's an area that Tony's started to appreciate further recently, especially since his role as assistant head coach of the Paralympics GB cerebral palsy squad. 'Having done my Goalkeeping Diploma in the last couple of years, I've really started to appreciate the importance of a goalkeeper coach that's connected and linked with their other staff members. When I'm working within my national teams, everything that I do links in with the overall playing philosophy and what is trying to be built. There are, of course,

differences from the cerebral palsy squads to the blind squads
and from goalkeeper to goalkeeper, but these are all within and
supporting the framework of the system that I'm delivering to.'

However, the role is not just the goalkeeper coach's. 'A
lot of work has to come from the outfield coaches, too: they
have to be willing to share and teach information about the
organisation, structure and philosophies of the club', describes
Tony. 'If I'm expected to deliver sessions with my goalkeepers
around themes such as set pieces, I need to understand the
playing system and intended outcomes on the field - it becomes
a menial waste of time if not.'

With the resources, money and time spent on outfield
coaching courses for goalkeeper coaches, Tony feels as though
there is a need for these knowledgeable and trained individuals
to have a more holistic role, working with the defensive units
and rest of the team within the training environment. 'If we're
assimilating and absorbing such a high level of information on
these courses, then why are so many goalkeepers coaches not
given the opportunity to act upon it?'

'Even when coaches do give their goalkeeping counterparts
a little bit of freedom to deliver with the defensive players, for
example, if there's any slight piece of information missing from
the exercise, the coaches will jump in as if they're lifeguards
and change the exercise or make an intervention. I always ask
about what would happen if the boot was on the other foot:

if the goalkeeper coach jumped into the outfield practice with such regularity, what on earth would the coaches think?'

Questioning Tony about whether there are any coaches who are striking the right chords in this sense, his response is one of understanding, but awareness of the work still to be done. 'There are some coaches who are excellent, and have the ability to step back and give a great level of trust to their goalkeeper coaches. Having said that, there are far too many who don't have the ability to delegate fully to their goalkeeper coach and allow them to have more ownership over the team. It's a shame, because there's so much incredible perspective and ideas that goalkeeper coaches have but, if the environment isn't right, they often won't leave the coach's thought journal.'

On how to change the situation, Tony is rather abrupt and incredibly explicit in what needs to occur. 'Certain individuals throughout the world of football need to get off their high horse and put away the ego that this culture revolves around. The thought pattern is "it's my team, my practice, my organisation and therefore I'll do everything". Quite frankly, it's not. It's a shared process between all of the backroom staff and the players, for the development of the team, squad or club.'

ELEMENT THREE

'Setting and remaining accountable to goals and objectives with your goalkeepers and planning for this within your programme.'

A growing phenomenon in the modern world of sport and performance as a whole, it is undoubted that goals act as motivators, objectifiers and measurers of success. Using them to the benefit of goalkeepers is imperative to a coach's achievement, and Tony's experiences working with Paralympic teams have amplified his beliefs. 'If you're going to achieve something, you will have goals - it's that simple.'

'The planning for the cerebral palsy qualification for Rio 2016 didn't start the year before the competition, there was a change of staff and we were brought in as soon as London 2012 was over.' Tony describes his journey with the cerebral palsy squad in more detail, venturing into how he and Keith Webb worked to create a goals-based programme. 'Keith and I were selected to manage the team, and there was a great level of trust put in our operation to develop players, qualify for Rio 2016 and ultimately have the opportunity to play in a medal match. I think it's a perfect example of goal-setting, because we had a variety of different layers of goals (mainly process and performance) and we knew exactly what was expected going into each major tournament, coming away from each training camp and even from each individual match.'

An England team has never placed as high as Tony's in the European or World Championships, whilst the progress made by a number of goalkeepers within the squad was exceptional. Every detail of the training, matches and performance was objectified, with specific goals and targets at every step on the journey to success. Ultimately, the squad qualified for Rio 2016, and came within whiskers of a medal, as we've already looked at, after facing two of the best teams in the world in Brazil and Ukraine. 'The history books will tell you that we lost both games 2-1, but no British team has ever got anywhere near that close to beating this kind of opposition. We plotted and worked towards getting closer to the big hitters within the world of cerebral palsy football, and many will say that we achieved that in the matches we played, even if it didn't quite have the final touch.'

Tony also sees, though, an important role for goal-setting at a grassroots level. 'It's all relative, without a shadow of a doubt. The goals and targets we're setting for our international athletes will be very different for the 10-year-old boy or girl who's putting on the gloves for the first time. At this stage, everything is being considered from a process perspective (can the goalkeeper catch the ball, move their feet or make a low-diving save?), but the idea of relativeness in goals is something that holds true throughout the system.'

'I speak a lot about working to challenge yourself and your goalkeepers to improve as an individual and have the opportunity to play against better opponents. For me, also, this has to build from the fundamental basics upwards: there's no point encouraging your 10-year-old from earlier to execute a side-volley, counter-attack distribution if they haven't worked out how to catch a ball that's moving towards them. It's the goals we set that allow players to recognise this journey, too, and the mechanisms that need to be in place in order for them to improve their performance and develop new skills.

ELEMENT FOUR

'Ensure goalkeeper training is specific and relevant to each individual you're working with.'

There's no doubt that no two goalkeepers are the same; there are so many individual variables that will separate one goalkeeper from the next. Especially at the elite-level where improvements in performance and development will be relatively marginal, having this appreciation for specialised and specific training, relevant to the needs of each goalkeeper, is crucial. 'I think the first thing I look at with a new goalkeeper is how I can assess their abilities and requirements for improvement', Tony says, after firing a plethora of questions my way that he may use to undertake this assessment. 'For me, it's less about the sport in this case and more about your connection with the individual as a person that will dictate whether or not you can recognise, and they'll be willing to share, the areas where development is most impactful. If you can't connect with your goalkeepers, and prove to them that you're going to do everything in your power to support them, how can you expect them to confide in you with their strengths and weaknesses?'

It's clear, for Tony, that first contact, impressions and building an initial sense of rapport with his goalkeepers is crucial to being able to understand their individuality and how training should be adapted to suit. Coach the person before the player, is the idea that comes to mind.

ELEMENT FIVE

'Ensure the goalkeeper is sufficiently mentally prepared for competition.'

Psychological understanding of goalkeepers in competition is a science that is growing rapidly, as many begin to see the importance and individuality of a goalkeeper's mental state. There are increased studies into areas such as arousal, managing emotion on the pitch and reflecting on performance. In Tony's opinion, a lot of the psychological fundamentals are the responsibility of the goalkeeper coach. 'The higher up the levels you go, the more psychology becomes prevalent in the goalkeeper's coaching programme. For me, that's the way it should be right from grassroots: there's much more to the position than just the technical ability to stop the ball.'

'Building a strong psychological goalkeeper isn't all about being positive and encouraging them to succeed', says Tony, 'but it's ensuring that they have the opportunity to experience the toughest situations that they'll face in the match and learn how to solve and respond to them. It might be that you reduce the level of information that you give to the goalkeeper, to force them into a match-like situation where they've got to think on their feet, or you step up the service to a level they can't deal with and that brings around a low success rate.' These moments in training and the environment are imperative to building a mentally tough goalkeeper, especially one that's ready and prepared for international football.

'At the same time, however', adds Tony 'you have to build up the confidence and belief of your goalkeeper positively. Show them that you care about their progress, that you're working together to achieve their goals and work on a lot of the skills we've mentioned in the relationships area of the book to really maximise and motivate the potential of the goalkeeper to work with you and achieve their goals.'

Most importantly, it seems as though knowing what to say, how to deliver it and when the moment is right is crucial in developing a goalkeeper psychologically. 'There are a number of scenarios where I don't think coaches quite understand this', replies Tony. 'When you've got a coach berating a nine-year-old goalkeeper for not coming off their line, and then the next ball over the top they wildly charge out and are lobbed, with the coach once more shouting fury at the decision, how does the little kid feel? You've got to question the coach's knowledge, competency and appropriateness to be coaching grassroots football at this point: how much does he understand about the damage he's doing to this young person's attitude of football, not just goalkeeping, potentially for the rest of his time on this planet?'

Mistakes are learning opportunities in any walk of life and, more often than not, the goalkeeper will be palpably aware of the issues he's being criticised for.

Goalkeepers are under large amounts of pressure in the goal from a very early age, and this is something that Tony feels is channelled in the wrong way for some, with the goalkeeper becoming a scapegoat to release general frustration and displeasure. 'An outfield player can mistime a pass, shoot wide of an open goal or give a clearance straight back to the opposition, but the slightest mistake from the goalkeeper and it's as if disaster strikes.'

This is, though, a part of the position and Tony understands that the goalkeeper needs to be able to deal with it. 'Through the very nature of their work, the goalkeeper has to be equipped with high levels of confidence, resilience and composure, but sometimes I think these are exposed unnecessarily, especially at the grassroots level, by uneducated and frankly dangerous coaches, who put someone's life-time affinity with sport on the line for the sake of feeling good about being a mini-Mourinho.'

ELEMENT SIX

'To advise and assist the selection of goalkeepers for matches.'

How suitably this fits into the 'ethos' of a goalkeeper coach may, at first, be questioned, but the reality of the situation is that it is searching and seeking a deeper level of meaning for the team dedicated to improving performance between the sticks.

'This is something that maybe isn't so relevant at the grassroots levels of the game, where coaches may be working with goalkeepers from different clubs and age groups in one session, but it's certainly a massive element for me in the elite game. The goalkeeper coaches are involved in the coaching setup for a reason: they have a specialised skill-set and a great depth of knowledge around the goalkeeper and their performance. If the goalkeeper coach is just involved to serve balls and collect a few kicks, I don't see the point on including them within the process - use a first-year scholar instead!'

'However, if the goalkeeper coach is there to provide technical and tactical support to the goalkeepers and first-team staff, assist and advise in the selection of the team and have a real integral influence on the goalkeeper's role in the game, then we're going to be able to get the absolute maximum from them.' Tony's quick to deny that the goalkeeper coach should have the final say in the selection process, but certainly believes they act as an imperative consultant through the mechanisms. 'The goalkeeper coach will know if a certain goalkeeper is physically, mentally, technically and tactically equipped in a game of football because of the experience and connection they've built up with the individual - this should be respected and appreciated.'

'It's down to the manager to take on-board their goalkeeper coach's suggestions, summaries and advice before they then go away to make the ultimate call. Some coaches will have particular preferences about the skill-set they require of their goalkeeper and that's not an issue at all, but the goalkeeper specialist should still be involved within the consultation process. That's pivotal, for me.'

As a goalkeeper coach working across such a combination of differently organised environments, though, Tony believes that the power in this area does not lie solely with the goalkeeper coach, and that there is more work those outside the position need to do to adjust their methods. 'The manager is fully aware of the incredible knowledge and analysis skills that their goalkeeper coach will have, yet I still see far too many situations where the goalkeeper coach is discouraged from sharing their opinions, belief and expert knowledge in a context where it could be crucial to a team's success. It's the manager's responsibility, more than anyone else's, to build that relationship with their goalkeeper coach where thoughts, ideas and recommendations can be shared openly in a two-way process.'

ELEMENT SEVEN

'Creating a culture where performances are assessed, analysed and actioned upon.'

When I challenge Tony on what creates this culture, his response begins, ends and revolves around one distinct word. 'Learning. Every time you play', Tony continues, 'you learn.'

'No two games are the same, and even when you glide through a 'clean game', there'll be something that the goalkeeper can pick up on to improve - or imitate - moving forwards. The role of the goalkeeper is so deep and there are so many variables involved that to say the goalkeeper could possibly have a 'perfect' performance would be ludicrous.'

For Tony, the biggest current issue is one of logistics. 'I'm in a position at the moment where there are so many responsibilities and plates to juggle that it can be hard to find enough time to really undertake a deep level of analysis. I miss that, to a degree, because it helps me to learn and develop as a coach, as well as my goalkeepers, and it's a very important part of my coaching and goal setting.'

Changes in recent technology, and the advancements that they have brought, also amplify the importance of analysis for the goalkeeping department. 'It's as much out of fear and wonder for what other clubs or organisations are doing and how they're using the information available to them as anything else. We have to make sure that we're at least matching them, and developing our analysis on a socratic level; technology plays a great part in that.'

FORMULATING YOUR IDEAS

Looking through Tony's ethos, then, it is apparent that there are a number of messages that reverberate through his beliefs and can help us to understand the mechanics and ideologies by which he acquits himself and his programmes as a coach. It is maybe most telling that he emphasises the goalkeeper's holistic development in nearly every area of this ethos: it's no longer good enough to have a great shot-stopper between the sticks, you need a player who understands and absorbs the game mentally, tactically and from a performance-based orientation, too. The goalkeeper coach plays a massive part in this journey, and so there's no better time than the present to start creating, or honing, your philosophies and ethos.

XIII
THE SYLLABUS STRUCTURE

Through Tony's time in sport, he has worked very closely with the creation and adjustment of various syllabuses to improve and better his goalkeepers. In this chapter, we will look at the two fundamental aspects of these syllabuses (the 'structures', if you like) that you can use to build your personal development programmes.

THE SYLLABUS WHEEL

Footballing coaches work off a variety of different models for talent development and progression, each with their individual merits and perceptions of the game. Tony's experience and findings across formats has led to his own creation of a holistic model for talent development, implying that no area is mutually exclusive of another and that each can be influenced through a multitude of different media.

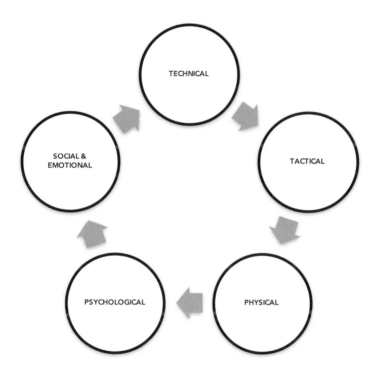

UNDERPINNING THEMES

'It's all relative to the goalkeepers you're working with and the level they're at, but this model works as the fundamental basis for me and I try to base all of my work off of it. There are a multitude of ideas in each element of the wheel and it's unrealistic to expect to cover all of these in one season, so it's all about prioritising what you believe your goalkeeper requires most and then adjusting your practices to suit.'

There seems to be great clarity across the organisations Tony's involved in with regard to his syllabus wheel and there's no doubt that it provides a methodical and focused approach to producing and developing goalkeepers. Over our many conversations, we've discussed the different areas that goalkeepers require particular emphasis on and I've started to appreciate just how individual the needs of goalkeepers are, even - or more aptly: especially - at the international level.

'There are still too many coaches, in my opinion, that focus exclusively on the technical side of the game with their goalkeepers. I understand and totally support that the technical side of the game is of paramount importance, but not every goalkeeper requires that as their primary focus, especially not in the elite reaches of the game.'

Dan James, one of the blind squad goalkeepers who will be featured in a case study later in the book, is a great example of this for Tony. 'Dan's been to two Paralympics, has an incredible understanding of the technical side of the game and is in great physical shape.'

'For him, we find that a lot of the work we do together is

around improving his focus and concentration for the game, as well as continuing to work on his in-game tactical appreciation and very specific technical adjustments. Many other coaches may be too concerned with the technical outcomes of the limited time they spend together, and so avoid breaking down the psychological barriers with their goalkeeper to really find out what's challenging them. It's massive for me. I find the holistic approach of the syllabus wheel imperative to sharing this viewpoint.'

At the end of this chapter, we have included an exclusive look at two different aspects of the syllabus wheel in application. Based around the futsal game, the first looks at priorities within each section of the wheel for goalkeepers, whilst the other considers the personal characteristics that would create an ideal goalkeeper.

INTERCONNECTED

Tony's design of the wheel is of particular importance when one considers the interconnected relationships between elements: they are most certainly not mutually exclusive of one another.

'If you notice, the arrows of the wheel travel to the circumference and go all the way around - it's an infinite process of development with all facets intertwined. It's imperative to me that we don't look to isolate one particular aspect of the wheel, as they all work together and we've got to have the ability to recognise this as their goalkeeper coach. Yes: I'll work on some areas more prevalently than others, but I'll try to do that whilst integrating a couple of different elements of the wheel within that.'

There's a reason that the wheel isn't prescriptive in its model and that's largely down to the way that the elements are connected, believes Tony, using the example of some of the world's greatest goalkeepers. 'Is Neuer the same as Buffon or De Gea? Absolutely not. They're all world-class in the way that their elements work with each other and the strength they've built up in each department. It'd be impossible to isolate each area and say "this is the absolute perfect model" because there are so many different variables with regard to the way the game is played. I have my idea of what I think the goalkeepers need as an overall development pathway, but the way they feed this into the other elements of the wheel, and the specifics behind each section, is totally based on their personality, capabilities and desires from the game.

THE SYLLABUS STRUCTURE

Now you've built up a knowledge of your philosophies as a coach, the ethics that you deliver that syllabus by and the holistic elements you're seeking to achieve, it's imperative to consider how your sessions can revolve around this. As with most aspects of his programmes, Tony allows himself and his coaches the creativity and ownership over their syllabuses, as long as they can comply to and be justified by four elements:

What - The areas of development that the goalkeeper needs to focus on. Where do these fit within the syllabus wheel and how are they relevant to match situations?

When - Are you working with the goalkeeper four days a week in an academy setting, three times a year at international camps or for one or two hours during training in the evening? Is this something you want to look at within match-play and analysis, or is it best suited to the training field and getting on the grass or court?

Why - What's the requirement of this in the game? Heavily based on the context of your goalkeepers, are we looking at creating the best U20 goalkeeper in the world or giving Tommy the best opportunity to enjoy football for his U12 team?

How - A mixture of all of the above, this is the methods and strategies which you plan to bring about these outcomes. What will be the focus? When will you work on it? How will you deliver your information to the goalkeepers in a way that they can learn, acquire and develop it over a long- and short-term approach?

This, in essence, is how Tony builds and delivers his long-term development programmes for goalkeepers. It's not based on a restrictive curriculum or the idea that all tasks will be the same for each goalkeeper. Instead, it focuses on building a framework of understanding for all of his sessions, so that each goalkeeper can be given individual autonomy and specialist practice as to what is most relevant to them. Needs may well change throughout the season. The flexibility of Tony's approach to delivering this information and developing the goalkeeper is no doubt why so many come away from his programmes as top-class, international goalkeepers, with the independence, desire and skill-set to continue their fight at the top of their format. In Tony's words: 'everything is about the why, and that will change for every goalkeeper you work with.'

PRIORITISED ASPECTS FOR A FUTSAL GOALKEEPER'S DEVELOPMENT

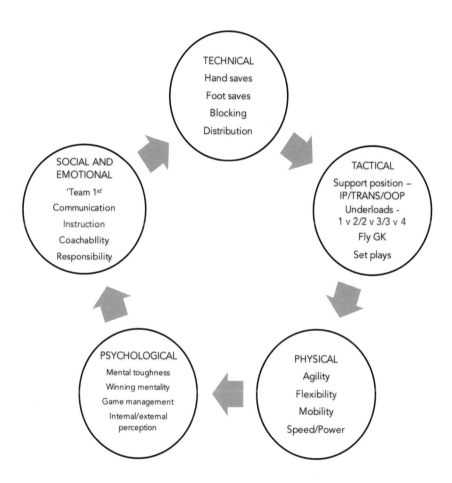

Once more, it should be remembered that this syllabus wheel can be adapted and moulded for individual sports, levels or formats of the game: use Tony's futsal wheel as an inspiration rather than a prescription for your personal priorities.

THE FUTSAL 'BIG ROCKS' FOR GOALKEEPING

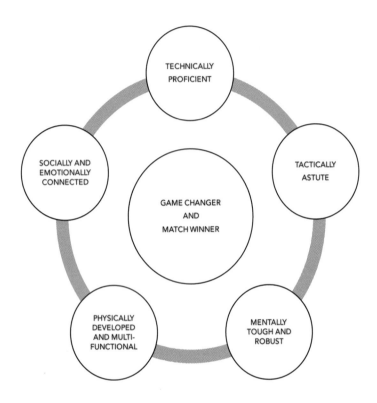

The 'big rocks' are the five components of a futsal goalkeeper that Tony believes makes them match-winners and game-changers. Again, we find ourselves in a situation where the big rocks could be easily manipulated (in-line with your personal philosophies) for each format and level of goalkeepers that you are working with. It focusses on Tony's five elements within the syllabus wheel, but could be extended to give real guidance to goalkeepers as to how they can improve their performance and development.

Section Four

Session Delivery

XIV
GOALKEEPER-CENTRED PRACTICE

Over the next section, Tony and I will discuss how he structures sessions in order to provide his goalkeepers with the best outcomes across his syllabus wheel, in addition to how the other elements of his philosophy integrate with the way in which he delivers his practice. Additionally, we've included a number of practices that you can tweak, adjust or use as inspiration for your own goalkeeper coaching - enjoy!

We start with an area that guides and channels the process, as a general theme for session delivery. There's a reason, says Tony, that he entitles his work 'goalkeeper-centred' and not 'Tony Elliott-centred'. It's clear that, with the abundant experience he's had within the game, he could design and deliver 1,000 training sessions for 1,000 different situations, create technical models of how a goalkeeper should play and have a pretty good idea of how to dictate analysis. Part of Tony's humility, self-awareness and understanding of development, though, drives him to a considerably different conclusion.

'I'm a coach, not a player. My goal is to help, share, and care. I've played the game and had some strong personal success within it, so I don't watch my players cross the white line to try and perform for me or because of me: it's their turn to take centre stage.'

As already eluded to, one element of this is to create individualised and bespoke practice environments. 'I could be very command- and instruction-driven in how I develop goalkeepers, but I think that'd detract from the main element of their development: they have to understand themselves, what they need and have the independence to make decisions off their own back. The collaboration between coach and goalkeeper is massive for me, especially as it becomes more apparent that the goalkeeper requires large levels of autonomy and ownership in order to succeed in their position.'

'It is a scenario where a balance must be struck, however', believes Tony, 'as there are some situations where outcomes are very necessary and we need to understand the cogs in the system to get there. During some training sessions, though, I will turn around to the goalkeepers and say "Look, we've got an hour... What would you like to spend it on? What areas do you believe need developing most urgently?".' By encouraging his goalkeepers to be a fundamental part of the decision-making, they start to understand their strengths, weaknesses and position much better: a vital tool if they are to continue developing at the top level.

Tony's experience and acumen as a coach supports him in facilitating a player-centred experience. He's built up a mental logbook of exercises, drills and conditions that can bring out a huge variety of different outcomes at the drop of a hat. Less experienced coaches, or those who are working in unfamiliar territory, may always choose to drop their goalkeepers a phone call in the days preceding a session to understand their goalkeeper's desires: the ownership remains at the forefront, but there's more planning in the way of delivering the session.

If there is one element by which a coach can undermine or build their reputation within the industry, it's through the physical, tangible and live sessions they can produce. With such a plethora of different ideas, opinions and philosophies as to the best systems for coaching athletes, sometimes the structure and style of sessions can be left behind.

COMPONENTS OF GOALKEEPER-CENTRED PRACTICE

Create a training syllabus to enhance individual capability

Shared vision between goalkeeper and coach

Challenge the goalkeepers according to the agreed vision

Allow each goalkeeper to reflect/review and come up with key elements in which they feel they need to develop in and enhance

Maintain constant contact with the goalkeepers so that joint reflection and planning can take place regularly

Observation is key during practice so that relevant feedback may be given to the goalkeepers regarding situations that occurred during practice

Practices to be filmed whenever possible to allow the goalkeepers further opportunity to reflect/review and to feedback

It is pivotal that practice is designed to enhance the individual needs of each goalkeeper so that the practice can then be linked to the game

XV
SESSION STRUCTURE

'The session's structure and framework is crucial to me', says Tony. 'There are many coaches out there who put on great sessions from week-to-week through their own individual ideologies, but they all boil down to a simple skeleton structure that can be easily transferred and adjusted.' Tony and I have spoken at some length about his individual styles of coaching already, so it is fascinating how this manifests itself in a tried-and-tested formula that Tony uses to build up his sessions:

```
P - pre-activation
A - activation
C - connection (technically-based work)
C - coordination (skill and match-realistic practice)
C - collaboration (game-based)
```

Covering each of these in a little more detail, it is clear to me just how flexibly they change depending on the context of the athletes and environment that Tony is working in.

PRE-ACTIVATION

Particularly changeable between athlete groups, Tony knows that the pre-activation is a pivotal area of a session for potentiation and injury prevention, but only when time and resources allow it to become a priority. 'I think that the pre-activation stage revolves around the context of who you're working with, the time at your disposal and the expertise you already hold. As a grassroots coach with 60 minutes on a floodlit pitch every Thursday evening, you're not going to waste 15 minutes of that session just on your pre-activation.'

'At the league level, on the other hand, it's the coach's job to manage and look after their players physically. We're responsible for any injuries that they pick up, especially if they're as a result of overloading or under-preparation, and that's probably why pre-activation is so big these days.'

It may sound like an overly-complicated scientific term, but the reality is - as Tony explains - it's just getting the body warmed-up and prepared for the practice it's about to face. 'It's all about preparing the player for that very first stage of physical activity. Personally, I like to use a lot of resistance bands, small dynamic exercises and even some free weights every now and again. We're looking at getting the blood flowing, the muscles on the move and beginning that idea of elasticity and flexibility that's a necessity at the top-level.'

I ask Tony, though, how he would adjust this pre-activation for a grassroots goalkeeper, and whether it can be made a more enjoyable experience. 'Especially if you're working indoors, I'm a huge advocate of the use of tennis balls, balloons, basketball or other, similar objects: they're stimulating for the goalkeeper to use, especially if you can integrate a game around bouncing or keeping them up in the air.'

'As I said earlier, we're just looking for exercises that get the goalkeeper moving, without necessarily over-stretching them. I use a lot of mini-tennis games now with the goalkeepers: it gets them lunging, changing direction, stretching for the ball and very quickly prepares them for the remainder of the training session.'

ACTIVATION

The reality of the grassroots level is that, often, the pre-activation and activation will merge into one another, but that's not a problem, as Tony explains. 'I generally like to refer to the activation phase as you're traditional warm-up, and within the grassroots game you do have to adjust your timings and may well include the pre-activation within your overall warm-up. If you're straight into contact with the football, that suggests to me that you've made it into the activation phase, and this is a point where it's of pivotal importance that you're using your resources to the best of your ability.'

'It's all about using your imagination and creativity to organise a simple but fun, engaging and preparative warm-up for the session that will follow.' We've covered a few warm-up examples in the session planning section, but Tony is a massive advocate of the use of multi-balls (basketballs, tennis balls, handballs) and these will often find themselves integrated into his warm-ups.

CONNECTION

'I use the term connection, in this sense, to talk about the build-up and structure of technical practice within a session: this is where I'm giving my goalkeepers the tools to be able to compete.' Tony's views on the technical phase are very much shaped around the ability level of his goalkeepers and the context of the session. 'I think you've got to be realistic. Personally, I start with minimal levels of information (but still ensuring this is realistic to the delivery and actions they will receive in a game), allowing me to get a feel for the goalkeeper's capabilities.'

'From here, I can very quickly start to introduce the goalkeepers to situations they're likely to be facing in a match. It's at this point that I'm starting to hope their thought pattern is along the lines of "This is a game - what am I going to do? What position should I take, how should I move my feet along the line and where is the ball going to be coming from?". These are the realistic questions that goalkeepers face every game, but I think we're too slow in this country to introduce them into our training practice and design.'

Tony also speaks with great enthusiasm about the importance of repetition through variation, an idea earlier eluded to. 'How many times in a game does a goalkeeper have to save a volley from exactly the same position?' Tony asks. 'Not many. Yet why does the majority of our service revolve around volleying the ball into the hands of the goalkeeper? It doesn't quite add up.'

'In order to combat this, it's as simple as serving the majority of the balls from the ground, whether static or moving, as this is where the majority of shots are taken from in a match. Have different service points, also, that force the goalkeeper to adjust their angles and perception is important - really focus on getting as much of that repetition through meaningful and contextualised variation as possible.'

It's clear to Tony that we should coach goalkeepers as the game is played: in a match-realistic, variable and chaotic environment - he builds upon this when talking about the 'conversion' element of his practice.

CONVERSION

Becoming the skills-based element of Tony's practice, the conversion section is, in essence, where information levels are increased and the goalkeeper has to maintain technical consistency, whilst also dealing with a host of external stimuli and variables.

'There are a multitude of different ways that I increase the information in my sessions, all geared towards increasing the stimulation for the goalkeeper and the difficulty of decisions they have to make. It might be things like changing the distances used, the angles towards the goal or the speed at which the ball is delivered - there's no end to the opportunities, in reality. A personal favourite of mine, also, is to use a multi-goal system, which might take away slightly from the realism but provides a great challenge to the goalkeeper in terms of their angles and positioning as the shot comes in.'

One of Tony's trademark practices, as delivered on The FA's Goalkeeping Conference in 2016 is the use of a four-goal system, with each goalkeeper in one goal and a couple of servers on the outside. Whilst, in its purest form, it has excellent returns for close-range blocking and building upon reaction to a loose ball, the underlying framework can be adjusted to create a very different practice with a totally unique set of outcomes, just by adjusting principles such as the space between the goals, the goalkeepers working at any one time or other alternatives.

COLLABORATION

Imperative to a goalkeeper's development, the collaboration phase is the opportunity that the coach and the goalkeeper have to work together in the context of a match-situation. The nature of this phase varies massively from grassroots to elite football, so Tony and I will tackle each of them individually, although there is no doubt that some aspects are transferable.

'When I'm working with a small number of goalkeepers in an isolated training session, it comes down to my preparation and understanding that I've been working on a specific theme throughout the session. If, for instance, we've been looking at playing out-of-possession when the defence is deep, straight away that suggests to me that we'll be looking at a shot-stopping collaboration, having to deal with the delivery and finishing of balls in and around the eighteen-yard box. The players may well have some ownership about what the final practice looks like, but it's all about reverse engineering the expected outcomes from the end of the session, and allowing them to be integrated into the collaboration practice as well.'

Stripping that down further, to a grassroots environment, and for Tony it's about keeping the play game-based. 'Far too often we see bus queues of kids, with the coach server the most active participant and the goalkeepers are just peppered every shot. Instead, why not try to provoke realistic movements and an underlying game-sense by playing 3v3s or 4v4s? All of a sudden, they're having to tackle and deal with balls from a host of different angles, with varying defensive positioning and shot styles from the strikers. Even beyond that, there are a huge number of games that help the goalkeeper to increase their contact time with the ball, and these have surely got to be more productive than lines of players waiting to have the ball whacked at them.'

The picture is different, still, in our final scenario, which is working within the elite game where the collaboration takes place in the whole team training, and the goalkeeper coach works alongside their support staff to continue to produce the required outcomes. 'At this point, the coach's perspective and line of vision has to switch. No longer are they just looking at the goalkeeper in the goal, but they're starting to understand, appreciate and analyse their position within the whole-team system. This is where the goalkeeper coach's expertise around a particular format comes to the forefront, and it becomes even more crucial that the coach can recognise the right moments to share this knowledge.'

'For obvious reasons, there's less live coaching in this phase: the goalkeeper has to focus on the game and understanding how and when he might influence the play. This means that the time you have to manipulate and work with the goalkeeper is very limited. It's all about making the decision to make the best intervention, at the best time with the best technical information relevant to the goalkeeper in that moment.'

'Sometimes', Tony adds, 'it's not necessarily about analysing in the moment of the game', and this is something that he believes coaches take a while to get used to. 'If we know and appreciate that there are maybe only two or three instances within the session where we can make an intervention, our focus has to be around mentally or physically noting down the areas that we'd like to discuss with our goalkeeper after the practice.'

'It's not an easy skill to master, without a doubt, and it

takes a lot of experience and learning to be at a point where you can recognise the when, the how and the why within the moment of the game. Too many coaches, though, love the sound of their own voice so much that they expose the players to far too much information at the wrong moments, and probably pay the price because of that.'

XVI
CREATIVE PRACTICE

Goalkeeper coaches have to be creative in the way they go about creating practices for their goalkeepers. So often, we see uniform, linear line-drills that serve little purpose other than non-functional movement patterns repeated week-after-week (anyone fancy some quick feet through cones?!). However, with our knowledge that we've now built about the need to adapt for individual goalkeepers, the importance of a match-realistic environment and our desire to be able to push our goalkeepers to the next level, Tony is determined to share some of the ways in which he manages to combine creative and pragmatic thinking to create sessions with excellent outcomes for the goalkeepers.

To start, he talks of the importance of creativity when working across various formats. 'Across all the formats I've worked, no two have been the same. The speed of the game changes, the number of players on the pitch changes and there are many other constraints that create a very different ball game when you're moving from one format to the next. For me, this has required such a massive level of creative thinking.'

'There are a few general areas that you can work with, but the majority of those returns will have to be tailored based on not only the individual goalkeeper, but also the format in which he or she is competing. If we take an example from the men's game, look at a goalkeeper's starting position. It's likely that he's going to be starting two or three yards down the line of the ball for a shot around 15 yards out, dependent on height. Now, in the women's game that'll change instantly, because the worry is that if the goalkeeper moves forward too high, they will be easily lobbed or leave a large area of the goal open for the opposition. Instead, we want that goalkeeper to drop deeper, maybe a yard away from the goal line.'

'However, the obvious fall-back of this is that we're now asking the goalkeeper to cover more space either side of her, and also directly above as well. What does this do? It changes the requirements of the goalkeeper. All of a sudden, we have to emphasise the vertical spring and ability to travel laterally across the goal, in addition to the power and drive to reach the far extremities of the goal. Immediately, that requires a re-calibration of the training that you're undertaking with the goalkeepers. Failure to recognise, adjust and creatively manipulate based upon that could be very dangerous indeed.'

The goalkeeper coach doesn't have to be creative in isolation, though. If the stimulus for their work is the requirements of the goalkeeper, then there are a number of support avenues they might use to build upon their thinking ability to create a session. 'It might not be that the goalkeeper coach can do all of this creative work alone, and I know there have been many instances where I might have tapped into the sports scientist, for example, to look at how we can maximise the outcomes based on the specific needs of the goalkeeper in a particular moment, especially if we're looking at something such as lateral movement or vertical spring.'

'The creativity is how you deal with the problem, or task, of keeping the ball out of the goal for the specific goalkeeper and the format in which they're playing. You can transfer from one format to the next, but that is minimal in reality. The role of the goalkeeper in the game is so specialised and so sensitive to change that the reality is that there are so many complexities in the game that goalkeepers need to be able to adapt to.'

IMMENSE KNOWLEDGE

As a starting point, this hopefully gives a greater insight into why creative practices are important (because the game rapidly changes) in addition to how you can begin to form your own philosophies and structures for undertaking this.

However, there are a couple of prerequisites that can smooth the journey and make the process easier. 'For coaches, to be able to build this platform of creative thinking, you need an immense knowledge of the game of football and how different elements of the game have varying impacts on the play. It isn't a case of clicking your fingers and then suddenly being able to create incredible practices; it requires years of immersion and knowledge-building, before you can then move forward to apply that with the individual goalkeepers that you might have in front of you.' Some might say that this connects quite well with Tony's opinions on intuition that we spoke about in the second section of the book.

'I give a lot of credit to futsal for this, because it really has helped me to become a creative, intuitive and independent thinker, purely based on the work that needed to go into the format when I first entered it and the desire it gave me for unearthing knowledge around the game and understanding how the different elements piece themselves together. Very quickly, I realised that there wasn't much out there in the sense of 'ready-made' practices, and therefore I wouldn't even have a fall-back plan. The only way to ensure that I could coach at the highest level was to digest, absorb and search for as much information about the game as possible.' It's from this knowledge base that Tony has managed to build and weave in his creativity. In sum, then: creative thinking is a necessity for goalkeeper coaches, but requires a strong knowledge base and an open mind to be most successful.

SESSION EXAMPLES

Below, Tony has included a number of his sessions that
he delivers across a number of different aspects. Through
looking at the progressive practice required for the forward
kick through technique to his infamous four-goal practices.

It is probable that you will have to adjust these practices to
suit your athletes: a first team coach, you may look to apply
and implement some of the technical themes discussed;
a youth development coach working with big numbers
of goalkeepers may focus on taking small amounts of
inspiration to implement their own non-linear and TGfU
practice designs.

They have been extracted straight from Tony's collection of
sessions and, therefore, are displayed and represented in a
variety of different ways.

As always, if you have any questions at all regarding the
practices, then you can either head online to see some video
footage of many of them in action, or get in touch via the
website and social media channels.

THE FORWARD KICK THROUGH SAVE

Forward kick through:

1. - A flat marker spot is placed approximately one or two metres from the goalkeeper (in a similar position to the ball in the picture below). The goalkeeper uses the spot for reference and attempts to lead with the foot towards the spot, driving the leg directly down to the floor, placing their opposite hand down behind themselves to buffer some of the impact on the ground as they fall.

2. – Progress the process now by having a ball held on the floor at arms length away from the goalkeeper's feet. The goalkeeper leads with the foot, driving it directly down towards the ball held firmly by the coach. The sole of the foot is used to make contact with the ball to push it directly back towards the coach. It is important that the goalkeeper gets used to and becomes proficient at using both feet when executing the forward kick through save!

3. – The goalkeeper now progresses from making contact with a static ball to working on their timing and making the correct contact on a moving ball that has been rolled towards them by the coach from a distance of one or two metres.

4. – The practice is now further progressed so that the goalkeeper must try to deal with a ball delivered towards them from a distance of four or five metres. The goalkeeper must now decide which foot to kick through with and this will be determined by the pace, line and flight of the ball.

Although the focus of the practice is the kick through technique, the goalkeeper must use the element of realism and use the correct save technique accordingly!

From this point, execution of the skill would then be progressed to inclusion in opposed and match-realistic practices, where coaches may consider using constraints or affordances towards certain areas of the goal to guide opportunities to use the technique.

DROPPING TO DEFEND THE GOAL FOLLOWED BY TRANSFERENCE OF BODYWEIGHT TO SAVE

Activation:

WARM-UP WITH BALL

ORGANISATION

The goalkeepers and the coach form a circle type shape and stand approximately four or six yards apart with one ball between them (spare balls at the side).

PRACTICE DETAIL

1.   The goalkeepers and coach attempt to keep the ball from touching the ground by only using the palms of the hands to do so.

2.   Only one touch of the ball per keeper is permitted until another keeper has touched the ball.

3.   Upon the ball touching the ground, the process is repeated.

PROGRESSION

1.   Only left/right hand.

2.   Compulsory two touches.

3.   Compulsory two touch - first touch with any part of the body, second touch with one of the hands.

4.   One touch with the hand whilst the group attempt to pass another ball between them keeping both balls constantly moving.

OUTCOMES

Hand-eye coordination

Speed of movement

Parrying/deflecting

Diving

Passing

Communication/information

Awareness

Reactive speed

Mobility

Agility

Connection:

FOOT SPEED, HANDS AND REPOSITIONING

ORGANISATION

A.   The goalkeepers work in pairs.

B.   Each pair work in a small goal four yards wide, with four differently coloured discs set out in a diamond shape in front of the small goal.

C.   One of the pair works in the goal, the other goalkeeper acts as server.

PRACTICE DETAIL

1.   On the servers call (front, back, left, right), the goalkeeper moves quickly to one of the discs and then returns to the centre of the diamond where they deal with a static serve.

2.   The goalkeeper saves as they see fit and the ball is either returned to the server if secured or the server uses a spare ball if needed.

PROGRESSION:

1.   The server calls a colour and delivers a moving ball.

2.   The server calls either front or back for a vertical movement from the goalkeeper and then one of the two side colours of the diamond for a secondary, diagonally forwards/backwards movement from the goalkeeper.

3.   The server calls front, back, left or right and the goalkeeper falls to the ground in that direction. The server then calls a colour and the goalkeeper recovers back to their feet and moves to the disc before returning to the middle of the diamond. A moving ball is now delivered by the server.

4.   The server calls either front or back followed by the two side colours in any order. The goalkeeper now makes a combination of forward or backwards vertical movements followed by a diagonally forward or backward movement and a lateral cross-step movement to get back into position to deal with the ball served. A multi-ball system may be used now.

OUTCOMES

Speed of movement (multi-directional)

Set position

Handling techniques

Diving techniques

Reactive speed

Mobility and agility

Conversion:

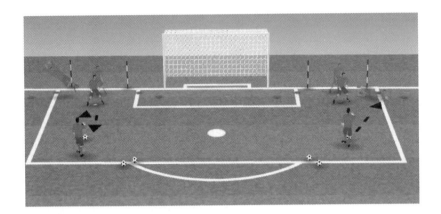

ORGANISATION

A.   The goalkeepers work in pairs.

B.   Each pair work in a small goal four yards wide, with two smaller one yard, diagonally forward positioned goals, off set either side of the four yard goal

One of the pair works in the goal, the other goalkeeper acts as server, standing approximately ten yards from the goal.

The goalkeeper working stands next to a flat disc, positioned centrally, four yards from the goal

PRACTICE DETAIL

1.   The goalkeeper and server pass the ball between themselves using one touch if possible.

2.   On the servers call, the goalkeeper drops off towards the goal line.

3.   The server attempts to pass the ball into one of the smaller goals to the side of the four yard goal and the goalkeeper reacts to the pass and attempts to save.

PROGRESSION

1.   The goalkeeper stands just off the goal line and the practice is repeated. This time, on the server call, the goalkeeper sprints out to the disc four-yards from the goal, drops off back towards the bigger goal but now the server attempts to score in either the four-yard goal or one of the two smaller goals to the side of the four-yard goal.

OUTCOMES

Recovery back to goal

Speed of movement(transitions) – Backwards/diagonally forwards

Set position on strike - triggers

Handling technique decisions

Diving technique decisions

Parrying/defecting

Agility

Mobility

Passing

Distribution

Collaboration:

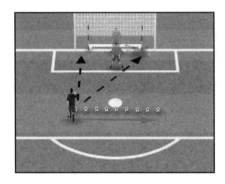 

ORGANISATION

A six-yard goal is created with two poles on the goal line of a full size goal. A line of balls is placed approximately 15 yards from the goal (a line of 12 balls is in place for a practice with three goalkeepers rotating after every strike).

PRACTICE DETAIL

1.   The goalkeeper stands next to a disc placed four or five yards centrally from the goal line.

2.   On the servers call, the goalkeeper drops off towards the goal line and at any time the server can attempt to score either side of the goal, using the space between the pole and the outside post as a target.

3.   The goalkeeper attempts to save using the correct technique depending on the type of ball delivered.

PROGRESSION

1.   The line of balls is moved back to between 18-20 yards and the practice is repeated.

2.   The server now stands approximately 25 yards from goal with a ball at their feet and attacks the goal at an angle with the ball. The server has a maximum of three touches before they have to strike at goal and can shoot from no closer than the edge of the box.

3.   As above but the server is now played through by another server standing three or four yards behind them.

OUTCOMES

Recovery back to goal

Speed of movement (transitions) – backwards/diagonally forwards

Set position on strike - triggers

Handling technique decisions

Diving technique decisions

Parrying/deflecting

Agility

Mobility

PROGRESSION

1.   The line of balls is moved back to between 18-20 yards and the practice is repeated.

2.   The server now stands approximately 25 yards from goal with a ball at their feet and attacks the goal at an angle with the ball. The server has a maximum of three touches before they have to strike at goal and can shoot from no closer than the edge of the box.

3.   As above but the server is now played through by another server standing three or four yards behind them.

OUTCOMES

Recovery back to goal

Speed of movement (transitions) – backwards/diagonally forwards

Set position on strike - triggers

Handling technique decisions

Diving technique decisions

Parrying/deflecting

Agility

Mobility

ONE-ON-ONES AND FULLY BODY UTILISATION (A BRIEF IDEA)

Dynamic system approach:

FOUR-GOAL SYSTEM

ORGANISATION

Four mini-goals are placed in a square approximately 12 yards apart and two servers place a supply of balls around the outside of the area.

The four goalkeepers stand in front of and defend one of the small goals each.

PRACTICE DETAIL

1. The two servers deliver the balls alternately

2. The servers can attempt to score in any one of the four goals

3. The goalkeepers attempt to protect the goal using and utilising all

parts of the body.

4.   If a goalkeeper secures the ball upon saving then they can attempt to score against any one of the other three goalkeepers

PROGRESSION

One of the servers moves into the centre of the area and the single server can still score into any of the four goals but they can also play into the centre server who can then attempt to score into any one of the four goals

OUTCOMES

Set position on strike - triggers

Handling technique decisions

Parrying/defecting

Lower-body saves – blocking/spreading/foot saves

Agility

Mobility

Flexibility

As discussed, whilst Tony most commonly uses this practice to work on blocking and spreads with a full-body utilisation, it could equally be transferred and adjusted using various constraints to focus on other areas. For example, using bigger goals and making the space bigger may probe more long-range shots, whilst taking out a goalkeeper in the current format might promote more lateral movement and anticipation of the ball direction (as goalkeepers have an empty goal they must cover between them).

Goalmouth exercise:

THROUGH BALLS

ORGANISATION

Three 'attackers' are positioned around the edge of the 18yd box.

Four mannequins, mimicking defenders, are placed strategically in front of

the attackers who must move around the mannequins when in possession

of the ball in an attempt to score.

Attackers A and B have the ball played into them whilst attacker C is

already in possession of the ball.

PRACTICE DETAIL

The server calls A, B or C and that attacker attempts to score once in possession of the ball.

The attackers must move around the mannequins when in possession of the ball in an attempt to score.

The goalkeeper attempts to get in position quickly and enter into a 1v11 with the designated attacker and defends the goal accordingly by choosing the correct save technique

PROGRESSION

N/A

OUTCOMES

Start position

Angles

Decision Making

General Shot Stopping

1v1s

Blocking/Spreading/Cross shape

Bravery

Speed

Section Five

Case Studies

XVII

DAN JAMES
(BLIND SQUAD GOALKEEPER)

Dan James has been involved with the blind football team since around the end of 2006, many years before Tony was involved with the squad. For those not aware of the format, the biggest area of significance for the goalkeeper is the fact that he is the only sighted player, and therefore has a large role around guiding and leading his team, in addition to keeping the ball out of the goal. When Dan and I speak, I note that I am speaking to a true professional, with integrity and independence in the way he works and conducts himself. This has manifested itself on the pitch over the years, with Dan certainly in the fight for being one of the best goalkeepers in the world inside the blind football format.

His gratitude towards Tony and their work together is also clear, and it's interesting to see how some of the aspects from earlier on in the book are touched upon by Dan during our interview:

'It wasn't until 2014 that I first met Tony, which is obviously quite a considerable length of time after I had started with the blind squad', says Dan when I ask about when the two first met. 'I'd actually attended one of Tony's futsal workshops in the past, because I was interested in looking at the transferable elements between blind football and futsal as a sport, so I certainly knew what Tony was about when he came into the setup.'

IMPRESSIONS

'My first impressions were clearly that Tony was the model professional, who took a great deal of pride and pleasure in the work that he was a part of. He would always arrive with sessions planned and was a massively organised individual. I had a great deal of respect for Tony right from the off, especially given his playing career as well, which I think helped us to relate with each other even further.'

'Our first opportunity to work together was on a training camp, where we were down to one goalkeeper on the programme and looking for a new goalkeeper coach to bring the project forward. He was introduced and I was delighted: it was great to have the opportunity to work with him from there.'

Dan's requirements as a goalkeeper, though, were probably a little bit distant from the normal expectations of a new coach. 'Tony would probably be the first to admit that his work with me didn't particularly focus around the technical aspects of the game, as I'd spent years building up that knowledge and skill set to make sure that I was in the best technical shape possible. However, where he really did add a lot of value was around the understanding of the constructs of the game, how to manage different scenarios in the match and how to cope with the fast-moving nature of the different phases of play.'

'It would be Tony's background in futsal that would have the greatest influence on Dan's technical proficiency. 'It was more the finishing touches and detailed technical movements, more than anything else, especially with those that we could transfer from futsal, as I was already pretty confident with the majority of the technical model. The forward kick through was also imperative, especially given that I'm 6"3 and a collapsing save isn't always the most appropriate, given the pace and intensity of the shots!'

Dan speaks about how they built up the forward kick through over time, which relates well to the previous plan in the 'Session Delivery' section of the book. 'We spent a lot of time and energy working on this, and it was a fascinating technical journey to go through. It was a very progressive practice, and I think Tony hit the nail on the head, which is especially impressive considering that he had to filter and reorganise all the futsal variables he might have previously considered in order to decide what was best within the blind game.

Clearly, though, Dan's best improvements came away from the technical domain. 'I used to be quite goalkeeper-centred on the field. Another area that Tony really pushed with me was trying to build my levels of communication on the pitch, to worry as much about the team as myself personally. The difficulty with blind football is that you've got to give the four lads on the pitch information at different points, but also to manage their emotions and make sure they're in the best frame of mind. Tony helped me to build up my confidence and belief in my ability to lead the team, without a doubt.'

CARE

Moving on, I ask Dan what he believes helped Tony to relate with and build a connection between them over the years. 'The biggest thing is that he cares.'

'Being a former professional goalkeeper, I think he

understands and could relate to me on a different level to some other coaches in the game, who that's maybe been a struggle with. I know that I could send Tony over a couple of video clips from work I've been doing outside of camp and he'd take the time and have the diligence to respond to that thoroughly, because we both wanted to achieve the best possible outcomes.'

'Anyone can put a session on and achieve some kind of outcome at that level, because the goalkeepers are striving to achieve intrinsically, but the level of detail in applying our training to the game and caring about the sessions was really what stood Tony apart.'

'He'd ring me up, I remember, and check in with me regularly so as to see how I was performing in my own personal training, because we obviously spent a lot of time away from camp. To have a coach take that personal interest in me was massive.'

'There's not a lot more a player can ask for than to know that Tony was always only on the other end of a phone call, should I need some advice or help, and also in the sense that he would be the first to come to me to share session plans or ideas for how he'd like to move our training forward. He's very open and honest in that he shares a lot of the stuff he does. A lot of coaches can be quite precious about their work and keep it private to themselves, but Tony's excellent because he's prepared and willing to share that information.'

Speaking of Tony's commitment to maintaining communication channels with Dan, I challenge him slightly on whether that should be the expectation for an elite-level coach. 'Tony's job with the blind squad was not a full-time one: it was to deliver the sessions on the camps, primarily, and give support around the tournaments as well. That's what made it even more striking for me that he'd spend so much time catching up with us over the phone or in person during the week, making sure that everything was moving forward OK and sharing the ideas that he wanted to implement', says Dan, with a real tone of appreciation in his voice.

'Things like that go an awful long way, especially in our sport where contact time might be limited to a couple of sessions a month, but where there are big international games constantly on the horizon.'

'Over the course of my career, I'm used to going through the motions with my coaches. It's an impossible feeling to articulate, but Tony and I just connected, massively, and were on the same wavelength with the way we wanted to be treated, how we wanted to represent ourselves, and the ideologies that we believed were correct to achieve this - it was a totally different experience to some previous coaches.'

'He gave me a massive amount of praise and respect, which is something I haven't been used to whilst playing. It certainly helped my ego and self-confidence, which perhaps is something that I've struggled with in the past. He wanted me to be the absolute best that I could be, and wasn't willing to compromise on that, even if it meant extra hours or training sessions on the field. All of a sudden, I felt a desire to play for Tony and train hard to work between sessions so that we could come back and work together to move forward in my development.'

MOMENTS

There are a number of memories that Dan speaks of to summarise the work of Tony in their time together, and they can give a real practical insight into how Tony managed the person, as well as the player, in a number of different scenarios.

'I remember one time we were playing against Brazil (the best side in the world) in Hereford. Tony had to leave early and couldn't make the game as he was working on a big project for The FA at the time, but I'll never forget how I felt going into that match. Tony had a brief word with me, told me to text him the score and that I'd get on fine in the match without him; it was one of the first occasions where I've really felt totally independent as a goalkeeper, and that I was truly capable of managing that game on my own.'

'We ended up holding on to a 0-0 draw, which was an incredible achievement for all involved, and I recall Tony ringing me up straight afterwards and saying something along the lines of "look, I'm not surprised. You've got to believe in yourself and what you're doing because you're a fantastic goalkeeper." He was chuffed to bits and absolutely made up for me, as well, which made a really poignant impact: Tony really did care about how we were getting on and our successes.'

Dan also speaks of the Seoul World Games, in 2015. 'The support that we had from Tony throughout that event was invaluable, both on and off the pitch. Whether it was in the analysis meetings, on the pitch or back at the hotel, you could always count on Tony to have your back and make sure you were as prepared as possible for the game ahead.'

'We were fortunate enough to reach the final of that tournament against Argentina, and I remember making a string of good saves through the game, until disaster struck with just a couple of minutes on the clock.' The team were 1-0 up and fighting for their lives, with an exquisite performance from Dan encapsulating their bravery and determination. He tipped the ball round the post for a corner, and at this point nobody believed that there was a return on the cards for the Argentinians. However, two quick-fire goals in the last 90 seconds sent the momentum of eruptions in the other direction, as the England side were suddenly sent to the floor, sucker-punched by the two late blows. England had lost 2-1.

'It was heartbreaking. There aren't too many other ways I can describe it. I remember how I felt after that game and it will never go away. Tony took me to one side after the game, whilst all the other players and staff were pretty much in pieces, and explained to me that "that's football: sometimes you don't get the rub of the green". He was devastated, too, but having that hand on the shoulder to show that he cared about me and our success as a team was really quite touching. He told me later that he went back to the hotel room and just cried down the telephone to his wife. That's how much we meant to him as a coach.'

A sobering thought, yet an invaluable insight into the working of Tony and the vividness with which going the extra mile remains.

FINAL THOUGHTS

It is clear that, as I ask Dan if there's anything he'd like to add at the end of our interview, he holds his relationship with Tony as one with close family. 'The bond I have with Tony is different to that of any other coach I've had. He's like a father figure. I looked forward to every training session I had, because I always knew that there was a learning curve ready to be negotiated and that there was more that I could potentially learn.'

'He's an outstanding coach, who understands people and the elements that make them tick. What's always impressive for me is the amount of knowledge that he's happy to share; he's such an open person in that respect. You can see that by the number of coaches that he's mentoring and supported through their journey.'

Figure 21: Tony (right) serving to Dan during a training session.

Figure 22: The silver medal from the Seoul World Games 2015.

Figure 23: Connection. At its very finest.

Figure 24: Tony (middle) connecting once more with blind squad goalkeepers Dylan Malpas (left) and Dan James (right).

XVIII

RYAN KAY
(CP SQUAD GOALKEEPER)

Another example of a goalkeeper that Tony has worked with, Ryan Kay has represented the Great Britain and England cerebral palsy squad in a variety of different competitions and events through the years (including Rio 2016). Held in very high regard within the game, both as an exceptional player and because of his career into the sport, he speaks of his journey into cerebral palsy football, his interactions with Tony and how these have influenced his life beyond sport, as well.

'I got into cerebral palsy football early in 2012, after my brother was scouted for the Nottingham Centre of Excellence playing another form of disability football', Ryan begins. 'He basically said something along the lines of "My brother's in the car and he's 15 years old - can he come and try as well?"... The answer was yes and everything developed from there really!'

Following a quick trial process, Ryan played his first game for the U16s a few weeks later, and was then invited along to the U21s' training session after being scouted by Jeff Davis and the England scouts, where things moved even more rapidly: he was called up to the senior side just a few matches later.

PLAYER-CENTRED

'The first time I met Tony was back in 2013 at Heathrow airport, before we were off to a tournament in Canada. Ryan remembers vividly the first thing that Tony said to him: "If I can make your life 25% better, both in football and beyond it, then I think we can call that a success". 'From that moment onwards', Ryan recalls, 'I had a mountain of respect for him.'

'Initially, the training with Tony was excellent. This surprised me as I think a lot of the staff expected that it'd take Tony longer to adapt to coaching disability players, but he got stuck in straight away and knew exactly what we needed to produce the best possible outcomes.'

'Everything that Tony did was to improve us as players and help the individual, in a player-centred approach. It was never about making Tony look good or flash: always about bettering us as players ourselves. Personally, we were looking at increasing accuracy and power within my passing, because it was certainly a weaker area of my game to start off with.'

Given the individual nature of the cerebral palsy format (where the severity and nature of the disability could influence different players at different rates), I ask Ryan about what steps Tony would take to ensure that the process was player-led and that they felt autonomy over their experience. 'Tony would give us a number of different options for how we'd like certain sessions to be delivered, along with guidelines of how he would recommend it, but it was excellent to have so much choice and to understand that everything that Tony did was to improve us based on our personal needs.'

'I liked how Tony would give us a number of options: it made us feel comfortable in the sessions and we always felt that we had a voice if we felt that something needed a slight tweak. He would never force me beyond my limits, and he understood that all individuals are different in their capabilities - especially in the cerebral palsy setup.'

'It would always be more about trying to find an alternative solution than labelling someone useless just because they couldn't make a save in a certain way.'

Having said that, though, Tony managed to maintain his professionalism and high-standards in his work. 'He was certainly disciplined and wouldn't allow us to slack off. Even if we were enjoying ourselves and having a laugh, everything was geared towards our goal of being the best 'keepers in the CP world, and Tony's professionalism really did shine through in that respect.'

Of course, the reality of the situation is that Tony's main goal is to be effective with the transition from training ground to match-day, especially with the technical grounding of many cerebral palsy sessions. I question on how successfully Tony managed this. 'The training transferred excellently into matches. We weren't doing things for the sake of doing them; everything was centred around match-realism and improving our skill set so that we could perform to the best of our abilities when we needed to. Everything had a meaning to it.'

'The ball was almost always moving, and coming from a variety of different angles, as well as having quite a lot of power, which was all realistic to the game we would play.'

MOMENTS

For coaches, it's not always the back page on which we make our headlines. Often, it will be the little conversations, the daily willing and the extra mile that we go that will define our legacy and how we're remembered. As Ryan recalls many experiences of games, training sessions and tournaments where his relationship with Tony has been exemplified, there is one conversation that lingers in Ryan's mind, beyond anything else.

'After the Paralympics, Tony and I had a conversation about the whole time we'd spent together, and remembered the initial conversation about improving my life by 25%. On reflection, there was a consensus between us that it had probably improved more than that: 40%, even. It was an incredible feeling and it makes me feel very humbled to have been able to be influenced and affected by him.'

It's this impact, this influence, that all of us invested in education and coaching surely strive for, with sport being the medium through which Tony has bettered those around him and left his mark on the planet.

Figure 25: Tony (centre) at a training camp with Ryan Kay (right) and Giles Moore (left).

Figure 26: Tony (centre) in Rio with Ryan and Giles prior to the Paralympic games.

Figure 27: Another Rio photo, as Tony spends time connecting with Ryan and Giles away from the pitch.

Figure 28: Ryan in his early youth, and showing what a development has transpired through dedicated work and opportunity.

XIV

JAMES WATKINS
(DISABILITY TALENT SELECTION MANAGER)

James' role with The FA is far-reaching and takes him into a plethora of different areas within the disability setup. He is spoken of highly by colleagues near and far, contributing massively to the development of disability football in the United Kingdom, especially in the recruitment and identification of talented young athletes who may be suited to move into the elite ranks of the game. Having know Tony on-and-off for an extended period of time, he seems particularly well-placed to speak about his work ethic, commitment to the cause and general persona.

'Ironically, I first met Tony when I was a schoolboy at Hereford', James tells me. 'I didn't know him well, but we were acquainted briefly at that age as he was a pro at the club and obviously we shared similar circles. We lost touch as we both moved on to pastures new, but I then connected with him many years down the line in my current role as The FA's disability talent selection manager.'

INITIAL CONTACT

And this relationship would be refined as a couple of the squads were looking for new coaches, who could adapt and deliver to the complex needs of the formats. 'Tony was doing a lot of work within The FA already, mainly with the England futsal squad, but we established that we definitely needed to improve the pathway and opportunities for our goalkeepers.'

'Tony seemed like an excellent individual to bring this forward, so we reached out and made that initial contact with him, to try and bring him on-board with the disability formats. I guess what we needed for our game was to transfer a lot of elements from futsal, because a large number of our disability formats are either futsal-based or follow a very similar structure; engaging with a coach who had experience working at the highest level in the country with futsal wasn't an opportunity that we could just pass-by.'

Once Tony was inside the system, though, James wondered initially if he had been slightly misguided. 'It was difficult to work Tony out at first because he was very much driven by his own philosophies and was clear about what he wanted to achieve, with that introverted facet to his behaviour as well. In the early days, I was possibly guilty of believing I would have to keep a real eye on Tony to ensure he didn't totally move away on a different tangent.'

'Soon, though, the strength he possessed as a coach flew to the forefront, and it was clear that his eagerness was merely the desire and passion he had for coaching and self-improvement, manifested within his emotions. It didn't take long to notice that he was very driven, he was very prepared, and he was ready to take on most challenges that could possibly be thrown at him. That's probably why he became so sought after, working across a plethora of different squads and developing a reputation for himself that made him quite a premium, really, to obtain access for your squad.'

ENGAGEMENT

James then moves forward to discuss the role that Tony played within the organisation. 'His primary role was to consult with our goalkeeper coaches, but the blank piece of paper we started with quickly filled itself up, with Tony navigating his way through an abundance of national and regional centres. One of the things about Tony that really struck me was his ability to constantly adjust his skills to suit the audience he was working with, whether that be in-service training, working across the national squads or supporting our younger goalkeepers.'

'I cannot speak highly enough of this area of his work: he has been exceptional in engaging with parents, players and coaches to really provide the whole coaching philosophy and experience that is maybe overlooked sometimes when they're working with so many different keepers.'

James can recall a particular example of this, after some feedback he had from a player's parent who was impressed with the lengths Tony had gone to in support of his goalkeepers. 'There was one instance when Tony was conducting a regional visit down in Chelsea', he recounts, 'with the primary objective of working with the goalkeeper coach to analyse a couple of areas of his coaching, and share some new information around a number of technical adjustments. At an earlier date, another parent had informed Tony of a community-based session taking place later in the day back up North, which Tony said he would attend at the time. Now, most other coaches would have sacked off the six hour drive through at least one set of rush hour traffic, but that just wasn't in Tony's character. Driven towards engaging and providing the best possible experience for both sets of young athletes, he delivered his session down at Chelsea to an incredible standard, before jumping back in the car, hitting the road, and making the second session some hours later. That left a big impact on the parents and kids involved, I know that much.'

STANDOUTS

Many people have spoken to me over the course of the book about what makes Tony such a sought after element within the goalkeeping world, but James' perspective is potentially the insight that engulfs all of these and provides the most weight. 'Tony's absolute passion for goalkeeping is incredible. It seems irrelevant to Tony whether he's working with an international first-team stopper or a 13-year-old goalkeeper, and this is something that can be slightly less common to see in this line of work. Also, he undertakes unbelievable levels of preparation, in meticulous detail, and this leads to an incredible quality and intensity within Tony's sessions. His service is spot on, as is his tempo, which culminates in a very strong goalkeeper session when combined with the technical detail that he provides the goalkeepers and the standards that he holds them to.'

'Even as a player, I remember Tony had incredibly high standards for himself and those around him, which could well have been a result of his schooling with The FA down in

Lilleshall: he's always been an incredibly driven character', says James.

'I can never remember thinking, that on any given day, at any given camp, Tony was having a bit of an 'off moment', where perhaps his standards had started to slip, because he has always been absolutely on the money from the quality of his sessions to their execution.'

'During his time with us, Tony has worked with the England blind squad goalkeeper Dan James (one of our player case studies); the instrumental change in Dan's performance since working with Tony has been breathtaking. The standard started to speak for itself in both training and matches, propelling Dan to becoming one of the best goalkeepers in the world for his format over a period of time.'

Tony's diligence and dedication towards providing excellence for his goalkeepers maybe took James slightly aback at first, although he quickly realised exactly what Tony was about. 'I didn't quite notice the extent of Tony's qualities when I first started working with him, and maybe it was a little bit of a pleasant surprise to see exactly how high Tony's standards were and his quality as a coach.'

'This was reinforced when we were working with Tony in a squad environment: he's a very unique character. He's often off doing his own thing, preparing his sessions, but with the absolute utmost respect for whoever the head coach may be.

He'll follow their ideas, calling them gaffer and just fitting into his role within the squad as seamlessly as possible. It's maybe not something we see so much in the modern game, so it's incredibly refreshing to see this old-style of professional footballer etiquette executed in its purest state.'

QUALITIES

Respect is certainly an underpinning quality for Tony, although that can probably be deduced from many of the chapters that precede this one in the book. James reinforces this, adding that 'Tony works diligently and passionately to acquire the respect of the goalkeepers he works with and he absolutely deserves every bit of respect he gets. He shows those around him a great deal of empathy and respect, as well as always being interested in self-improvement and continuous learning.'

It's this self-improvement and desire to life-long learning that has contributed to many of Tony's successes over the years. James epitomises that journey, though, as he talks about the progress that Tony has made in the disability game. 'He's come from a position where, when he joined us, he self-admittedly didn't know too much about the world of disability football, and yet now he is the only coach in the country to have worked across both the squads simultaneously at international level, despite the formats having their distinct differences and characteristics for the goalkeeper coach to consider. It is testament to his ability to absorb, gather and analyse information, before abstractly applying it to the individual constraints and requirements of each game in itself.'

'Tony's appearance can sometimes make him come across as a no-nonsense, tough, giant of a man. Anyone who gets to know Tony, however, understands very quickly that he is, in fact, the polar opposite', replies James, when I ask about the impression that Tony left on other coaches within the setup.

'He's incredibly caring and quite sensitive, but you do have to make that initial connection with him in order for that side of Tony to let itself show. His genuine desire is to make a difference, which is probably what gives him the enthusiasm he has on a daily basis. There's no hiding the fact that he is a huge family man with an underlying desperation for, and dedication towards, supporting his family - probably more so than anyone I've ever worked with before.'

'Tony's rarely distracted with anything other than creating an honest living for himself that he can use to support his kids and wife, Tracy, who obviously hasn't been too well over the years. I think that's partly why he earns some of his kudos from various individuals: he can be away for large periods of time coaching abroad or at a tournament, working his socks off but, as soon as he returns home, he's supporting his family and trying to give them the best help he physically can.'

STYLE

We've spoken in great depths and detail throughout the book as to the nature of the goalkeeper's position, and the commentary that Tony gives to support and aid the best performance possible. To give a real insight into Tony's working practice, though, James shares some ideas about Tony's coaching style and how this contributes to the coach he is today. 'I think that Tony is somewhere in the middle of the continuum, if I'm honest. He has a real clear vision about how he believes that he can improve the goalkeeper, but he absolutely allows this to be influenced by the individuals he's working with: there is a complete culture of sharing in Tony's environments.'

'Often, his relationship with goalkeepers off the field and away from the camps would be just as strong as that on the grass, and I think that helped Tony ensure he was on the same wavelength as the goalkeepers when looking at their development and progress. In particular, it really helped to shed some light and a bit of insight into the age-old goalkeeper union: he was a real advocate of that and did everything he could to engage with the goalkeepers and build a strong relationship.'

But it wasn't just the time Tony spent as a specialist goalkeeper coach that James could start to understand his methodology from. 'On the cerebral palsy front, Tony was obviously the assistant head coach as well. He had that ability to influence the outfield players, and was never afraid to 'muck in' with the rest of the team; I think that speaks volumes about his confidence to deliver, as well as the integrity with which he's researched into the whole game, as opposed to solely focusing on goalkeeping specifics.'

'It's true that this says Tony is a massively adaptable individual: if you give him any kind of objective or goal, he'll work towards it without complaint and always relishes the challenge to further his skills and knowledge.' There is real conviction in James' voice as he says this.

'It all comes down to that absolute passion for the game. He hasn't just isolated himself with the mainstream format', James adds, 'and it's rare to see this multi-dimensional approach within coaches these days, because he's absolutely got involved where he could with the disability programmes and the female setup, too. Being able to move like that, across formats on a daily basis, is truly testament to his adaptability and inherent ability to remain professional and have great consistency in his quality of delivery through sessions.'

'There's always a feeling that Tony wants to be on the football pitch and have grass under his boots. He's all about getting the tracksuit on and working with goalkeepers, to the point where he used to make jokes about me just being an 'administrator' when I'd turn up pitch-side, purely because I was in a management role and therefore spent a bit more time in the office!' These are memories that James remembers with great fondness, and that typify Tony's dedication to working with his goalkeepers day-in-day-out. 'I do smile when I think about that - his desire to always be out there with goalkeepers has been something that has stimulated, challenged and enthused me many times in the past.'

TANGIBLE DIFFERENCE

For a pair of professionals who have known each other since their playing days, it is impressive to see such a great level of mutual respect between Tony and James. Over the course of our interview, James and I spoke about abundant experiences showing Tony's personality and mind-set; only some of these could make it through to the case study. It's this close bond and relationship that the two have fostered over so many years that adds the most weight to James' final remarks.

'In my opinion, goalkeeping is an aspect of the game where the goalkeeper coach can come in and make a tangible difference to the performance of their players. There are probably very few goalkeeper coaches, in reality, that do what

Tony has done, show that passion towards the cause and are able to inspire players to the level that he does - he should be very proud of that.'

XX

PETE STURGESS
(FORMER ENGLAND FUTSAL HEAD COACH)

Merely mutter the name 'Pete Sturgess' within the realms of youth development circles, and you will find that your stock has already increased four-fold. Working with Tony as head coach of the England futsal squad, Pete has since moved on to become the national lead coach of the Foundation Development Phase with The FA. The two bonded heavily during their time in the futsal format, though, and Pete tells us a little more about his experiences with Tony and the impression that remains today.

'When I started with the England futsal team, Tony was already the goalkeeper coach and had been in his position for a few months, engaging with the players and building up a relationship with them. There wasn't much of a decision on my part to continue working with Tony when I came to the forefront of the team's structure, purely because of the way he interacted with the goalkeepers and the diligence he had.'

'It was a no-brainer to keep him involved with the programme; you just can't get rid of staff like that', adds Pete, when I ask him further about whether there was any thought of a changeover.

'Tony will be the first one to admit that he was still learning about the game of futsal when he took the position, as he does whenever he ventures into a new format, but the passion, energy and enthusiasm he brought into ensuring he was at the cutting edge of goalkeeping development in futsal very much helped him to stand out from the others. When I left the squad last December, the work that Tony was creating and undertaking with his goalkeepers was on par with anything that you might find, even within the hotbed of talent across Europe and beyond.'

I ask Pete, first, if there are any particular goalkeepers that benefited from Tony's work within the futsal game. 'One of the biggest impacts Tony had was on a young goalkeeper, James Dalton, from Tottenham, that we picked up because he was considered "too small" for the mainstream sport of football. Over time, Tony converted James into one of the most consistent and highest-performing goalkeepers in this country (as well as across many parts of Europe).'

A great success for a new coach in the sport, Pete recounts the experience. 'It was almost as though all of the new techniques, strategies and philosophies that Tony had been learning were being filtered down to James as the goalkeeper, and James' development went absolutely through the roof at this point.'

LEARNING

Learning and self-development is a theme that has featured heavily throughout the book, so it feels appropriate to seek Pete's experience of how Tony worked when coming into the unknown wilderness that was futsal. 'When I started with the England job, there was some tried-and-tested information out there on the internet, that was relatively accessible and available to a wider audience: it was probably something that we were dependent on for the very short-term of venturing into international futsal.'

'However, Tony wanted to put his own stamp on the agenda. He did this by taking on-board the information that was present, watching the game of futsal in its purest format, devising creative and innovative practices, and then assessing, or reflecting, on what worked and what was maybe not so successful from there.'

It would be this drive that would lead to the goalkeeper syllabus being created for the sport, but Tony's role wasn't exclusive to the athletes in the net. 'With the outfield players, we were developing a similar, games-based approach, and Tony was right with us through his goalkeepers and absolutely on the same philosophical level - that's probably the reason our relationship worked so well. In camps, we'd be training three times a day, which meant that we had the facilities for Tony to come in early and do a session with the goalkeepers, or for us to integrate some goalkeeping-specific practice within our actual coaching sessions. The way that the camps were structured gave us a lot of flexibility, and it was a big strength of Tony's to work within that. The players would still be deeply engaged during this period, and they were always being pushed to the very peak of their performance level.'

CONNECTING PLAY

This suited, it would seem, Tony's coaching ideologies and the way he wanted to structure his practice. 'Tony very rarely, if ever, works a skill in total isolation. Without compromise, he will find a way to connect phases of play, or link periods in the game together, so that the goalkeepers can appreciate the context of their movements in relation to matches. I think that this is an incredible tool for the goalkeepers when they step out onto the court, as they're prepared for responding effectively and correctly in matches, as and when they need to, because of the game-realistic scenarios that they've already faced on the training court.'

As Pete and I discuss this, it becomes apparent that Tony is a true practitioner of the learning and information that he absorbs. I ask Pete if he would agree, and whether he would attribute this mindset to any particular quality.

'A real strength of Tony's, absolutely, was has willingness to execute the knowledge that he'd learned with regard to the futsal domain, especially in the case of some of our young goalkeepers', reflects Pete on the rate of James Dalton's development. 'Often, coach education is at risk of not being transferred into actual coaching sessions, but a huge benefit of Tony's was his ability to take what he'd learned and share this information with his goalkeepers, however it may manifest itself. At the same time, he had the humility about him to accept that he wasn't the most knowledgeable futsal coach in the world at that moment, taking time out of his schedule to go across to Spain and other parts of Europe. He'd work with their goalkeeper coaches and absorb as much knowledge as possible, purely to see if he could improve himself and his goalkeepers' games in any marginal way. There was absolutely no compulsion behind this and it was totally because Tony wanted, and was eager to learn.'

'The relationship that Tony built with the coaches at Barcelona was incredible. Their futsal team is held up as probably the best in Europe, and Tony had an incredible relationship with all of the coaches at the club, particularly the goalkeeper coach. I know that this will have been a result of Tony's manner in approaching the organisation, the way he conducted himself when he was out there, and his willingness to learn. It will have endeared him to them, helping that relationship to grow. It's something that Tony gets everywhere he goes.'

When I probe Pete further on this, his reply resonates deeply with many others that I've spoken to throughout the journey of this publication. 'Tony is very prepared to help anyone, and this attitude is often reciprocated five-fold by those around him. It gives Tony a lot of the opportunities to learn and grow as a coach and I would say that it's very much a product of his character and personality.'

Once more, we're looking at a situation where Tony has immersed himself in a game and its individual constraints, before he then creatively forms his own opinions. 'As his confidence improved, he then started to formulate his own thoughts and devise his own sessions, ideologies and opinions as to the best methods for producing and developing goalkeepers depending on the situation.'

It's fair to say we all go on this journey: at first, we need a mentor to guide and instruct us, intervening as appropriate, and then over time we develop the understanding and inclination to formulate our own thoughts on situations and how we believe they are best dealt with, building confidence as you go. Pete gives particular credit to Tony's ability to do this whilst at the pinnacle level of international futsal.

ADAPTIVE EXPERT

For one of my final questions, I ask Pete how he would summarise Tony as a coach, and what qualities underpin him. 'We would call Tony an adaptive expert. This means that he takes on new information quickly and can see almost instantaneously where it might fit within his ideologies, implementing it if he believes it can support him as a coach. He's very flexible in moving with new trends and he's at the forefront of the game in that respect.'

'His enthusiasm and depth of knowledge speak for themselves and are really evident when we're on court... If a session was supposed to finish at three, you can almost guarantee Tony'll still be working with his goalkeepers at four unless anyone's told him to get off the court and give the keepers a break!'

Beyond the passion and ability to adapt that we've

already seen feature heavily through the book, there is also a resounding idea that Tony is a player-centred coach, who always puts his goalkeepers' development and success at the top of his priority list. 'Tony would always guide the goalkeepers towards the insight behind their own development: he's not the kind of coach to say "I've got all the answers", but instead he'll seek for the players to find that themselves, as part of a two-way process.'

'I think it's absolutely crucial to give the players autonomy over their own learning. It's incredibly difficult at the highest-end of performance, but I don't believe we should limit players to just being as good as the coaches knowledge. Development has to mean something to the player as well - when it does, it becomes so much more powerful. That was something Tony was exceptional with.'

CLOSE FRIEND

'Having someone who thought along the same lines as me', replies Pete, when I ask him how he would summarise Tony as a coach and a person. 'He always wanted the same things for his goalkeepers that we'd instilled throughout the rest of the programme, but at the same time remained humble in the position that he held: he could've very easily taken a lot more of the credit for the performance of the goalkeepers that he worked with. His emphasis really was the development of the team.'

'I have the utmost trust in Tony. I was always confident he was preparing the goalkeepers for the game they were going to play, at international level, and doing so in-line with our vision and philosophies about where we wanted to take the team moving forward. The outcomes and products of Tony's work speak for themselves.'

'I would consider Tony a very close friend that I can confide in, and that's a two-way process as well. All of that, though, has been built off the foundations of trust and camaraderie kindled through good times and bad within our journey together. We've never, ever, had crossed words, and we've always been fully supportive of each other's ideas.' A fitting tribute to a combination that helped lead a team to the most success the England futsal side has ever had, and set the foundations in place for the excitement that seems set to proceed them.

Section Six

Still hungry for more?

GK Icon

GK ICON

GK Icon was formed by former Premier League goalkeeper Richard Lee in 2008 with the idea of bridging the gap between grassroots and the professional game. Having been acquired by Challenger Sports in 2014, Richard and the team have seen GK Icon grow into one of the biggest goalkeeper brands globally. They aim to provide goalkeepers of all abilities the opportunity to experience regular world-class coaching delivered by professional coaches within superb facilities. Sessions focus not only on the technical aspect but also the tactical, physical and psychological side of the game: all critical ingredients in GK Icon's drive to maximise the potential of every goalkeeper.

When looking at top goalkeepers of the modern era, they all share certain attributes that make them world-class. Solid technique on handling, distribution, agility, speed and the spring needed to move around the goalmouth. The best goalkeepers also have the presence needed to fill those around them with confidence, knowing that they have a capable, calm and assured figure behind them, not to mention arguably the most important attribute a goalkeeper will possess: the character to deal with the ups and downs the life of a goalkeeper is sure to experience.

GK Icon offers an environment that guarantees increased confidence, skill level and, of course, plenty of fun! Over the coming year, Tony will be working alongside the business in more detail, with an integration across the growth of the brand into futsal goalkeeping.

For more information on GK Icon sessions, to keep updated with Tony's developments with the brand or to access GK Icon's exclusive glove range with Tony Elliott, visit **www.gkicon.com**

GK Nexus

Over the course of the book, I hope that you have heard in great detail about my constant and unrelenting desire to continue learning and plying my trade throughout my years in the game. At times, this has come with great struggle: resources simply haven't been available nor relatable to the requirements of the goalkeeper.

With my new GK Nexus relationship, though, all of this will change. We are working in tandem to provide relevant, explained and outcome-driven resources for your goalkeepers across a plethora of different formats, ability levels and environments. We will explain the 'why' and the 'how' behind our sessions, as well as providing in-depth information as to how you can transfer them to your training. If you're still eager to continue building up an incredibly detailed knowledge set and practical base to your goalkeeper coaching, I urge you to take advantage of the GK Nexus package today!

Allow us to take you on a journey, that will undoubtedly take your coaching knowledge and skill set, to the next level.
You can interact with our vastly experienced team of professional, UEFA Licenced, Goalkeeper Coaches, as they bring you the very best of content on a weekly basis.

To sign up to our GkNexus Members Area, please visit:

www.gknexus.com/members/tebook

Your first month is FREE- what are you waiting for?